Understand

SW

in a Day

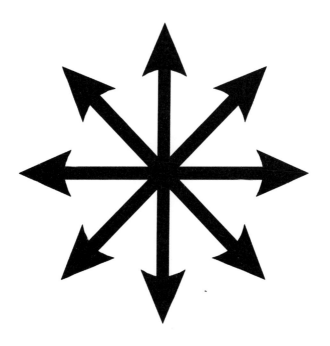

TTL

TTL is an imprint of
Take That Ltd.
P.O.Box 200
Harrogate
HG1 2YR
ENGLAND

email:sales@takethat.co.uk

www.takethat.co.uk/books.htm

You should take independent financial advice before acting on material contained in this book.

TTL are always keen to receive ideas and manuscripts for new
financial books. Please send details to the address above.

ISBN 1-873668-74-0

Contents

Acknowledgements

In the last two years, my life and career have undergone enormous transformation, primarily through becoming a NLP Practitioner. The insights acquired, together with lasting change mean that I now relish the next 50 years! The facilitators of that change have been my wonderful life partner, Heather Summers, and my teacher, mentor and NLP Trainer, Dr Susi Strang. Thank you to both and the friends and family who encouraged and supported me. The book is dedicated to them. The journey continues!

Terry Carroll, June 1999

About the author - page 122

Chapter 1

Background
Origin and definitions

A swap is a means of changing the nature of an underlying interest rate or currency risk, by exchanging currency, interest rate or both, liabilities or assets.

A currency swap is an agreement to exchange a fixed amount of one currency for another at an agreed rate on a fixed date, together with a simultaneous agreement to reverse that transaction at an agreed rate on a fixed future date.

An interest rate swap is an exchange of interest rate commitments. It is the equivalent of a long-term loan and a simultaneous matching deposit. It allows a company to fix its interest rate payments or receipts in advance at a known rate. Interest rate swaps usually involve the payment by one party of a fixed rate of interest and the payment by the other of the prevailing floating rate LIBOR rates for a three-month, six-month or any other such period agreed by the parties. Originally they tended to be related to liabilities, but have since evolved to include asset swaps and other esoteric products.

Evolution

Some say that interest rate and currency swaps have been around since the 1920s, but their emergence as one of the foremost financial risk and balance sheet management tools has really been since the early 1980s.

Their origins can be traced primarily to the foreign currency markets. Every exchange of currency liabilities or assets essentially involves interest rate based deposits, except where the transactions are on a spot basis. It was inevitable, therefore, that because currency swaps involved interest rate swaps within their construction (because interest rates tend to be at different levels from one currency to another), interest rate swaps developed a life of their own in the 1980s.

Before foreign currency swaps, where corporates did not want exposure to foreign currency risk, they might swap all such exposures into their base currency, or, in relation to future liabilities, purchase the currency forward, believing that they would thereby neutralise the risk. As you will see, as this text develops, any decision not to hedge a financial risk is tantamount to taking a risk (where there is a 'naked exposure') and indeed, because hedging involves taking a conscious, usually rational decision, passive acceptance or ignorance of risk is by definition speculative.

The beginning of financial risk management

We shall discuss the concepts of transaction risk, credit risk and default later. It will show that, without insurance or hedging credit risk, there will always be a financial risk where currencies, interest rates or prices are involved. The keystone of this book therefore, is the maxim of risk management: awareness, analysis, evaluation, management or insurance of risks, rather than abdication to fate! Barings and other cases have shown that no corporate can afford to be ignorant of, indifferent to or cavalier with, financial risk, especially in contemporary volatile markets.

As an alternative to neutralising exposure through instantaneous exchange of currencies, bankers and corporates alike developed the alternative of arranging back to back or parallel loans to manage the exposures related to currency based assets and liabilities. This was cumbersome and, without the chance coincidence of a corporate counterparty having exactly opposite exposure, would have to be arranged with a bank, who could stand as intermediary, exacting a handsome arbitrage fee for their troubles.

Markets have exploded in size and complexity since, especially in the use of derivatives, despite the 'causes celebre', to the benefit of international trade and global markets. More than 95% of foreign currency transactions are speculative, rather than being purely for the purposes of trade and, whether for speculative or financial risk management purposes, the interest rate and currency derivatives which are leveraged off the back of these underlying markets, have exploded at an even faster rate.

Currency Swaps

The currency swap market really started to emerge in the 1960s and grew modestly until the 1980s, when interest rate swaps were recognised and emerged in their own right. In 1980, the volume of swap activity was almost non-existent. By the end of that decade, the total outstandings of all swaps exceeded $2 trillion. Only four years later, the total volume of all swaps and swaps-related derivatives had grown to over $10 trillion, including over $1 trillion currency and $8 trillion interest rate swaps. By the year 2006, it is estimated that the total volume of all derivatives will exceed $500 trillion and will dwarf USGDP by 40 times.

By the early 1980s, the term 'swap' started to come into common parlance in financial markets. At first bankers made the running, as their corporate customers were approaching them to seek help in removing currency risks, especially for short to medium term liabilities. Bankers responded by acting as intermediators, for a fee. Soon afterwards they quickly recognised the opportunity not only for another revenue stream, but also to manage their own portfolio of financial risks. They moved on to hedging the risk, during the period it took to find an offsetting counterparty. They were also able to take advantage of their privileged position in understanding credit and counterparty risk and juggling the portfolio of 'mismatches' between various clients' requirements.

The banks with the broadest spread of global interests and mature operations in all the major currency markets were able to make the early running. The rapid growth in numbers and scale of operation of international banks in the two decades since is a testament to the growth in foreign exchange speculation and currency derivatives, as much as it is to the growth of world trade in general. The latter has been massively facilitated by the growth in the flexibility and scale of the swaps markets.

Portfolio management and the new derivatives

By the early 1980s, many banks were managing their swaps on a portfolio basis and, based on the parallel emergence of mathematical models for evaluating financial risk (e.g. Black-Scholes), were becoming highly sophisticated in understanding the opportunities, as well as the risks.

It was inevitable that, as this growth in sophistication was matched by volumes, the 'rocket scientists' who appeared would invent other esoteric products. This not only dramatically increased the efficiency of markets, but also contributed to the explosive volume growth and underpinned the now mature science of financial risk management.

While swaps became a mature mainstream risk management tool, documentation also became standardised. The Eurobond markets (existing wholly 'offshore') also exploded as a means of readily raising liabilities, because of the ease with which the currency and interest rate risks could be swapped. It was often substantially cheaper to issue a swapped Eurobond than to borrow funds domestically, especially where overseas credit risks were more attractive in one market than the domestic market. As a result, the swap markets became highly liquid (despite not being traded).

Manufacture of interest rate risk products

Swaps were so successful that the term 'swap' came to characterise the management of interest rate risk by the end of the 1980s. It became readily recognised that every treasury related product (except spot foreign exchange and its derivatives) involves interest rate linkage. The banks enhanced their revenue streams and balance sheet efficiency further by understanding the interest rate components of every risk, stripping them down to basics and manufacturing products to precisely meet clients' needs. This was especially attractive for non-standard commitment dates (i.e. other than 3,6,12 months)

It wasn't long before sophisticates saw interest rate and currency commitments as 'strips' of principal, or 'quasi-principal' (interest) payments. This triggered the proliferation of zero-coupon and deep discounted products, together with asset swaps, deferred transactions and the other esoteric swaps and derivatives which are now commonplace (such as the swaption). By the end of the decade, therefore, banks were using derivatives both for product and treasury management purposes. It wasn't long before corporates caught on to the highly leveraged opportunities for revenue generation, as well as hedging their balance sheet and financial risks.

Growth continues despite disasters

By the mid-1990s, there had been a catalogue of consequent disasters, in which the corporates were not in splendid isolation (as the banking losses following the default of Hammersmith and Fulham Borough Council were to demonstrate - see later). In 1995, the UK's oldest bank, Barings, had become a victim of what the Governor of the Bank of England, Eddie George, called "the dreaded derivatives". Even so the growth of derivatives, including swaps, has continued apace, despite the global concern of central bankers at the leverage and size of these 'off balance sheet' instruments. Indeed, while Barings demise was due to speculation in Japanese Equity derivatives, lack of control over the exposure may have been almost as much to blame.

Swaps, like other derivatives, are a means for transferring risk between counterparties at the most efficient price (or there would be arbitrages). They also dramatically enhance market efficiency and unlock cash and other resources that would otherwise remain under- or unutilised.

It should be recognised that even if the most gloomy predictions of world financial disaster which were rife after Barings were to come to'pass, it would be more likely to be ignorance, gaps in regulation, or lack of management, which would be at the root, rather than a particular tranche of derivatives exposures which failed. We shall also refer later to the Gibsons Greetings Cards and Bankers Trust case study, where ignorance by the customer combined with the bank taking advantage to produce one of the more infamous cases.

It is easily overlooked that in the late 1980s, Hammersmith & Fulham B.C., hopelessly overexposed to rising interest rates, as a result of entering into 'barrow-loads' of interest rate swaps, checked the situation with their lawyers. They found that the swaps contracts were '*ultra vires*' (beyond their powers or authority) and simply repudiated them, at a cost to the balance sheets of scores of reputable banks. Despite the repercussions, the market absorbed the losses and has continued to sail on.

Swaps have changed our financial prosperity

At the outset, in the old days, swaps worked because of the theory of comparative advantage and consistently produced "I win-you-win" scenarios. Now that the counterparty is more likely to be the portfolio of treasury risks of a bank, arbitrage has reduced swap transactions to financial evaluations and judgements of risk. Swaps have enhanced banking revenue streams and also supported the development of products that we now take for granted as commonplace (such as fixed rate mortgages). As a result, ordinary householders are effecting interest rate swaps, by moving or rearranging their mortgages. Furthermore, fixed and guaranteed rate savings products are now equally commonplace.

Swaps have come a long way. In company with derivatives in general, they have become highly sophisticated. Regulation is evolving to ensure recognition and management of domestic and global risk. Understanding is evolving. The problems are not in the instruments themselves, which have facilitated the growth in world trade and the quality of life of many countries in the world. They may also have added to the volatility of markets on the way. They are part of the mainstream of financial society. We can learn from occasional mistakes and grow in sophistication, to our mutual benefit, for swaps and derivatives are not going to go away. Indeed they now dwarf the volume of world trade and total world GDP.

Whilst they do not have the same flexibility as other derivatives (especially the market traded instruments, such as futures and options), swaps have become one of the main ways by which corporates and bankers alike can manage their balance sheet, currency and interest rate exposures. It would be no exaggeration to say, therefore, that the sophistication of markets and of many users is now such that almost any exposure or cashflow stream, denominated in all but the tertiary currencies, can be managed, hedged or translated into any other exposure or stream, through interest rate or currency swaps alone or in association with other derivative products.

Chapter 2

Understanding Financial Risk

A lthough interest rates and inflation in the late 1990s are returning to the sort of levels last seen in the 1950s and 1960s, we live in an era of great volatility. Starting with the two oil crises in the 1970s and following through to the October 1987 crash, we have become more used to wild fluctuations.

The growth of volatility

Yet, despite the vast growth of financial instruments leveraged off equities, bonds, currencies and interest rates, the 'crash' of 1997, was shrugged off within months. Authorities have become concerned about the growth of computer-generated transactions and programmes and a huge amount of invested funds increasingly tracks indexes. But we have learned to cope and not be phased by a 200-point fall in the market that might have previously produced screaming, gloomy headlines.

Left unconsidered or unmanaged, the sort of financial risk resulting from such volatility could become a nightmare for corporates. The huge growth in derivatives may be a head-ache for central bankers, but financial risk management drives it. And its size ensures sufficient liquidity to hedge almost any exposure. It is abdication or ignorance of risk that should concern us just as much as naked speculation in instruments, which by the nature of their leverage, take volatility to new levels.

At a mundane level, interest rate and currency swaps have become 'bread and butter' for corporates in managing the daily business. It was swaps, which first spawned the growth of derivatives that have mushroomed to such an astonishing scale. These derivatives are not only available to protect corporate profits and shareholder value, they have also become major revenue streams for banks. Without them the scale of global trade and capital investment would be dramatically lower.

Exposure

Classically, there are three general types of exposure arising from foreign currency transactions: transaction, translation and economic exposure. **Transaction exposure** arises because a payable or receivable is denominated in a foreign currency. **Translation exposure** arises on the consolidation of assets and liabilities denominated in foreign currencies. It has sometimes been called accounting exposure. **Economic exposure** arises because the present value of a stream of expected future cashflows denominated in any currency may vary due to fluctuating exchange rates. These are, in general terms, the main financial risks arising from foreign currency transactions or exposures. They are only the tip of the iceberg in terms of all the financial risks that a corporate or bank may face, let alone those specifically related to swaps (or any other derivative).

Foreign exchange risks are only a subset of the holistic financial risk that an órganisation may face day to day. They arise because a corporation has assets, liabilities, negative or positive, actual, expected or possible cashflows. None of this takes account of the risks implicit in operating in competitive international markets. For example, there may be a huge pricing risk. Suppose a UK car manufacturer is selling into Germany. If the Deutschemark weakens, the UK manufacturer's selling price in Germany may have to change, resulting in lower local sales. If the Deutschemark strengthens, the UK manufacturer may be able to reduce prices and receive the same amount of sterling, but the local manufacturer's imported raw materials and parts costs may fall also. Each of these can upset the bottom line for the UK producer, as a direct consequence of foreign exchange fluctuations, before a penny has been received, let alone the effect on the amount remitted to the UK (translation risk).

Hedging is very often undertaken to neutralise transaction risk, as corporate finance directors like to work with certainty, even if it means foregoing the opportunity of a foreign exchange 'windfall' gain. For the same reason, they will often seek to fix the long-term cost of capital, maybe using interest rate swaps to do so.

Categories of Financial Risk

It is not the role of this book to consider all the financial risks that may be faced. However, many of them may arise through, or be capable of being hedged by, foreign currency or interest rate swaps. The following list is far from complete, but is annotated in relation to the relevance to swaps:

● **Interest rate risk** - the risk that interest rates may fluctuate before the unwinding of a transaction or commitment, adversely affecting the net worth of the business (we shall consider later, the concepts of duration and Value at Risk - VAR).

● **Currency risk** - the risk that currency values may fluctuate during the period of commitment, expectation or exposure.

● **Equity risk.**

● **Commodity risk**.

● **Financial instrument risk** - the risk that the current or expected value of a financial instrument may fluctuate or disappear altogether.

● **Cash flow risk** - the risk that cashflows may not materialise as expected, or in the value expected.

● **Opportunity cost risk** - the risk that the cost of not taking a particular action may be greater than the return on the chosen action. The most obvious example is a passive attitude to financial risk, whether through ignorance or irresponsibility. The decision to do nothing about the possible depreciation in value arising out of interest rate or currency changes is, by nature, speculative, as the costs of protecting such value may be much less than the consequences of not doing so.

● **Concentration** - the risk that overconcentration on a particular group of liabilities, assets, customers, suppliers, counterparties, etc may lead to a disproportionate loss when market conditions change (too many eggs in one basket).

● **Counterparty and default risk** - the mature role of bankers in creating or intermediating swaps has reduced this, as usually the credit risk of a bank defaulting is much less than a corporate. However, as those same banks experienced when Hammersmith & Fulham repudiated their liabilities in hundreds of swap contracts, the cost of default can be huge. It is the risk that an interest, currency or principle payment is not made on time or at all, because of difficulty or failure of the counterparty.

● **Settlement risk** - is related to the possibility that initial or final settlement is not made on time, or goes astray completely, due to failure, suspension or default in the settlement process. Even late payment can be hugely expensive if another party legally repudiates a contract as a result, due to no-delivery. The cost could be exaggerated during periods of high volatility.

● **Collateral risk** - collateral is assets pledged temporarily or permanently, to secure a liability or borrowing. If an institution issued and swapped a securitised bond and the economic circumstances of the underlying property market changed adversely, causing widespread default of the individual securities, the issuer may have difficulty making or sustaining the swapped payment stream.

● **Dealing risk** - this includes the possibility that the individual who agreed the deal, had no mandate at all, or was operating outside such mandate, as Nick Leeson did.

● **Credit risk** - related to counterparty and default risk. Generically, this is one of the most significant risks associated with swaps and other derivatives. It depends on such factors as the credit worthiness and risk of default of the other party, together with market volatility, which in the case of substantial exposures can dramatically change a party's ability to deliver performance of obligations on time and in full. Credit ratings are under constant review through rating agencies, but also through banks and other interested parties. Banks particularly, other investors, counterparties and some corporates will have credit limits for individual and grouped categories of risks and counterparties. It is important to consolidate all specific risks across the organisation, including parent and subsidiary company exposures. Derivative counterparty exposures would be aggregated with investment exposures.

● **Product risk** - risk arising from complex derivatives transactions, especially where swaps are included. It is important to constantly evaluate the risk implications of each individual element.

● **Basis risk** - this can exist where the interest rate or currency basis for liabilities is mismatched with the corresponding asset. It also exists where the hedge and the underlying instrument are mismatched, including differences in the maturity, interest rate or currency basis.

● **Hedge programme risk** - a financial risk related to a payment or stream of payments may have been hedged by a programme of swaps, which, at a point in time, match the duration of the payment stream. As interest rates or currency rates change, the duration may change, leaving a basis exposure. Not all swaps are neat 3, 6, 12 month, etc matches.

● **Liquidity risk** - the risk that there is not sufficient liquidity to effect the desired swap programme to exactly match the financial exposure.

Financial Risk Management

Financial risk is merely a subset of holistic business risk. The Risk management process is:

- ✔ Define and analyse the exposures;
- ✔ Identify the specific exposures;
- ✔ Evaluate and measure the identified risks;
- ✔ Manage, monitor or consciously and rationally decide to ignore the risk, keeping the potential value under constant review;
- ✔ Assign accountability for implementation and review;
- ✔ Implement the agreed decisions;
- ✔ Constantly review specific and general risks, with a view to reinforming the above process.

Financial risk management is at the strategic and tactical level. Holistically and specifically, financial risks can undermine, severely damage or destroy the company's net worth. At a strategic level, overall objectives, policies, guidelines and delegated accountability will be decided. At a tactical level, the individual swap decisions will be evaluated, taken, implemented, reviewed and reported to the strategic level.

Marking to market or fairly evaluating exposures on an ongoing basis, enables the holistic understanding of the change in net worth. Duration analysis is discussed later. Net exposure, and therefore, net worth can change dramatically *intraday*, let alone from day to day. Treasury systems need to be sophisticated and sensitive enough for someone with overall responsibility to keep exposure under constant review. Separation of function between decision and administration is also fundamental, as Barings and others also failed to realise.

Where interest rate and currency swaps coexist, it is important to separate out the effects of the separate movements, within swaps and across programmes and portfolios of swaps. It is all too common that the left hand does not know what the right hand is doing. An exposure may be hedged in one part of the balance sheet that leaves an exposure naked in another part of the business.

While many parties may be affected by change in specific interest rate or currency factors and there may even be industry risks where all companies in an industry are exposed to the same sort of factors at the same time, financial risk is highly specific to an individual organisation. No matter how sophisticated the product, FTSE100 or Glaxo futures cannot replicate the circumstances of SmithKline Beecham, despite them both being pharmaceutical companies.

Market risk is the risk that changes in a whole commodity, industry, currency, interest rate, swaps etc market may have an effect on specific financial risks in an individual bank or corporate. The Hammersmith & Fulham swaps default led immediately to swaps being suspended for building societies and public authorities, while everyone worked out whether these organisations had been operating beyond their authority in entering into swaps contracts.

This made it very difficult for all treasuries to operate in swaps markets as domestic and international interest rate swap liquidity was substantially reduced. It also affected overseas confidence in a range of other exposures, credit risks and instruments and the ability for the affected institutions to raise money in international money markets, especially Eurobonds.

Value at Risk (VAR)

Value at risk can be considered at the micro, macro and meta level. It seeks to calculate the maximum loss that a corporate or bank could sustain, on a probability basis, if a particular financial risk materialised, i.e. specifically an open position on a hedge or financial exposure.

At a macro level it calculates the total exposure to such positions and at a meta level, the overall net effect of unhedged financial risks on the net worth (and ultimately the market value) of a company or bank. Together with duration, it is a powerful technique both for evaluating total exposure and improving the effectiveness of financial risk management.

While mathematical models have been around for some time, the development of a holistic, cross-firm, cross-instrument, cross-exposure approach to estimate the potential loss in market value, is valid both for bankers and corporates (especially where the latter are so active as to effectively be 'traders' in the financial markets).

Chapter 3

How Swaps Work

Interest rate swaps

Short dated swaps tend to be priced off futures and longer dated off government bonds. Banks operating in the short-term swap market will deal at either the bid or offer side of the swap market, but corporates have to pay more, to include the cost of the higher credit risk and the intermediator's fee for arranging. In the longer term market, swaps are freely quoted as spreads against a range of Gilts in the UK or Treasury Bonds in the US. The swap cost is then the sum of the equivalent bond yield and the quoted spread. The graphs below show the movement in 10 year UK and US swap spreads between 1991 and 1998 (source: *Greenwich Natwest Derivatives*).

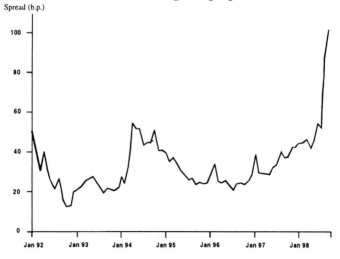

10-Year Sterling Swap Spreads

10-Year US Dollar Swap Spreads

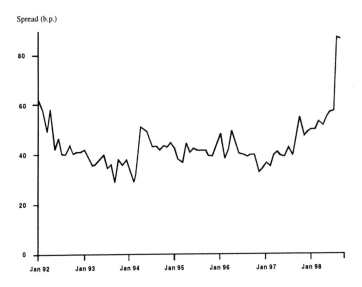

Calculating the cash flows for interest rate swaps is straight-forward, once the basis has been agreed. A corporate may have obtained initial funding on either a fixed or floating rate basis and swapped the interest rate basis to end up paying on the opposite terms. The general method for valuing an interest rate swap is described below.

So, for example, if a corporate raises 5 year floating rate money at 0.5% over three-month LIBOR and swaps it for fixed rate payments at, say, 7%, receiving, say 0.25% over LIBOR, it notionally ends up with fixed rate borrowing at 7.25%. Its payments will be at 7% pa every six-months to the swap counterparty and 0.5% over the LIBOR rate set three-months previously, every three-months, against which it will receive 0.25% over the same LIBOR rate, netting a cost of 0.25% to add to the 7% fixed rate it is paying.

Principles of simple valuation method for interest rate swaps

1 Valuing the swap when 'today' is a rollover date (i.e. swap payment date):

   a Interpolate the swap rates from the current yield curve;

   b The simple market value of the swap is the present value of the difference in basis points between the initial swap rate and the above rate, paid per period (semi-annually or three-monthly, as initially contracted), discounted at rates along the current yield curve.

Using the interpolated rate rather than the actual yield curve tends to result in a lower market value and of course the value of a swap does not change in a strictly linear way as interest rates change. Accordingly, for swaps contracted well away from the current rates, the difference will be more marked.

2 Valuing an interest rate swap on other than a 'rollover' date. To do this, one needs to disaggregate the elements.

   a Take all the cash flows occurring after the next rollover date and, using a method similar to the above, calculate the notional cash sum equivalent using the next rollover date as the 'present value' date;

   b Calculate the known future cash flows due on the rollover date (based on the existing terms of the swap from the last rollover date);

   c Calculate the present values of (a) and (b) above, using the method above and add the two amounts together, to give the overall swap value at a non-rollover date.

Note: the above are simplified methods for calculating the 'mid-life' value of outstanding swaps. However, a termination value should be calculated to reflect the market cost of terminating a swap, i.e. replacing all of the cash flows in the market place. Swap valuations are increasingly important to corporates in a world of increasing volatility and balance sheet changes. This becomes more so when one factors in exchange rate swaps.

Valuing exchange rate swaps

Making the point once again, that the methodology used here is more simplified than that produced by sophisticated computer generated models and/or used by bankers' traded portfolios, the following gives an outline of the method for valuing currency swaps.

The basis of a currency swap is usually the exchange of interest payments in two different currencies, together with an exchange of principals at the swap maturity. Although the latter will normally reverse an exchange made at the commencement of the swap, this is not relevant for the valuation, which only involves the remaining cash flows, once the initial swap has been made. As for the interest rate swap, valuations are made in terms of the net present values of all the remaining cash flows, made at the prevailing interest rates and exchange rates.

The method is to value all the cash flows due on the next interest payment date, add this to the present value of all the cash flow streams from that date to maturity and then bring the total back into net present value terms on the valuation date.

Method:

1 The present value of a principal amount and accrued interest received at the end of a LIBOR fixing period must always be the principal amount, irrespective of the rate of LIBOR, as the latter is used as the discount rate.

So, assuming a dollar/sterling swap of, say $10 million, at three-month LIBOR both ways, to 31 December 2002, with quarterly fixes, the present value of $10 million invested to 31 December 2002, from 30 September 2002, at three-month LIBOR, is $10 million (i.e. $10 million plus interest at the 30 September three-month LIBOR fix, discounted back to the 30 September at three-month LIBOR). By deduction, therefore, the present value of $10 million (and all associated interest payments), refixed three-monthly to 31 December 2002, discounted back to 30 June 1999 is also $10 million.

2 Similarly, the present value of the swapped sterling principal, say £6 million, and its associated cash flows, discounted back to 30 June 1999, is also £6 million. However, to this we have to add the up front margin payment. So, the present value of all the cash flows from 30 June 1999 is the net of a receivable of $10 million and a payable of £6 million plus margin.

3 These can be discounted back to the valuation date, say 14 May 1999, by applying the cash rates in dollars and sterling for the respective amounts, discounted back for 47 days and converted into dollars at the prevailing dollar/sterling rate on 14 May 1999.

4 We can then calculate the value of the dollar interest receivable at 14 May 1999 (three-months interest to 30 June 1999 at the previous dollar three-month LIBOR fix) and the sterling interest payable (three-months interest to 30 June 1999 at the previous sterling three-month LIBOR fix), convert the sterling payable into dollars at the 14 May 1999 dollar/sterling rate and net the two.

5 Add all the now 14 May 1999 converted, netted, present value amounts together and the total NPV is the value of the swap at 14 May 1999.

6 To value on a rollover date, simply delete step (4), above, using the same general method.

Swap deposits or foreign exchange swaps

Swap deposits have been known as interest arbitrages. It may be generally believed by the uninitiated that it is possible to borrow cheaper in one country than in another, because the interest rates are lower. So, a UK corporate, currently paying 6% for one year money may be attracted to the possibility of paying 3% in the 'Euro-zone'. If this were possible, the banks would have arbitraged away the difference some time ago.

The simple explanation is that, once you have exchanged the currencies into a common basis, i.e. sterling, the effective rate will be more or less the same, as explained in the calculation below. There may be a small advantage, making it worthwhile, but this is more likely to accrue through changing the interest rate basis, say from fixed to floating rate.

Formula for swap deposits

The simple swap deposit formula is:

$$\text{Interest differential} = \frac{\text{Swap x 36,000}}{\text{No days x Spot}} + \frac{\text{Euro\$ x Swap}}{\text{Spot}}$$

(Source: *Treasury Management,* ed. Hudson, CIB 1994)

Example: Sterling/Euro swap

A bank has received a £1 million six-month sterling deposit at 5.5/32% (quote: 5.5/16% - 5.5/32%). It does not require sterling at present and could only lend on in the market for the same term at the same rate, less the administrative and dealing costs of the transactions. It decides instead to use the funds in a Euro loan for the same period at, say 2.17/32% (quote: 2.19/32% - 2.17/32%), thereby matching out a potential currency exposure at the same time. Assuming a spot Euro rate of 0.66 (£/€) and six-months forward of 0.67, the calculation of the currency swap is:

Cost of £1 million for 180 days @ 5.5/32%

$$\frac{\text{£1m x 5.15625 x 180}}{100 \text{ x } 360} = \text{£25,781.25}$$

Therefore, the cash flow at maturity (principal plus interest) will be £1,025,781.25

Based on the current spot Euro rate, the bank could sell £1 million for €1,515,151.52 Using the forward rate for 180 days, it could buy £1,025,781.25 @ 0.67 at the same time, against the Euro, i.e. €1,531,016.79 to exchange the interest plus principal at maturity. In order to break even on the deposit, the bank therefore needs interest of:

$$
\begin{array}{r}
€\,1,531,016.79 \\
€\,\underline{1,515,151.52} \\
€\quad\ 15,865.27
\end{array}
$$

Using the formula for simple interest, the rate is:

$$
r = \frac{I \times 100 \times 360}{P \times T}
$$

$$
r = \frac{15,865.27 \times 100 \times 360}{1,515,151.52 \times 180}
$$

$$
r = 2.094\%
$$

Consequently, if it lends the funds in Euros at 2.17/32% (2.53125), it can make a turn of 0.437%.

Chapter 4

Interest Rate Swaps

To put it crudely, interest rate risk is the risk that movements in interest rates will adversely affect a corporate or bank's net worth.

If only life were so simple! There are two overall risks: that interest rates as a whole may move; that the shape of the yield curve will change. What the latter means is discussed later.

A movement in interest rates is characterised by a change in base rates, which will have an immediate impact on three-month and shorter rates and probably out to one year. It is also likely to change the shape of the yield curve, as any change in base rates tends to have an effect on market expectations as to: how long the rate will hold; whether the next rate change will be up or down. If expectations are for continuing falls, the yield curve may flatten. If for future rises, it is likely to become steeper.

Of course, different rate structures and yield curves exist in different financial centres and expectations in one can affect those in others. So, expectations of the future pattern of US rates may affect global expectations, especially in Europe, and vice-versa. It should be remembered, however, that interest rate differentials are equalised out through differing exchange rates.

Another definition of interest rate risk is that associated with applying different bases of interest rates to the assets and matching liabilities of an organisation, whether because there are basis mismatches (e.g. fixed to floating); or duration mismatches (e.g. different term liabilities funding different term assets).

We shall discuss duration later, but between duration based asset/liability management, swapping the interest rate basis of assets or liabilities and hedging the shape of the yield curve (also through swaps), a corporate treasurer or banker potentially has the tools to neutralise interest rate risk. When the possibility of using other derivatives, such as FRAs, options, futures and esoteric variants is considered, all things seem manageable.

Whether by accident or design, in the past, both corporates and banks have ended up with the 'bankers' folly' on their balance sheets; short-term borrowings funding longer term assets. Whether by nature or consequence, the liabilities were very often variable in rate, as against the fixed nature of the asset. If based on a deliberate judgement, this would be a cute strategy if interest rates fell steadily, as incremental revenue would accrue from the reducing cost of the liability being less than the fixed return on the asset. All too often, however, the situation was circumstantial and a rise in interest rates damaged corporate wealth.

Now, banks may have the human and electronic technology to predict and calculate possible scenarios and the consequent financial outcomes. Neither corporate FDs, nor their shareholders, however, appreciate fluctuating profits, apparently at the whim of markets and mismanagement. That's why interest rate swaps became so popular. They not only enabled the raising of more and cheaper medium term borrowings, but they also enabled the FD to enhance the certainty of profit.

It is a fact of life now that bankers and some corporate treasurers deliberately mismatch interest rate assets and liabilities, based on a view of the short to medium term outlook. Sometimes it is to make trading profits, sometimes it is to delay, for example, the fixing of a swap to secure the widest margin, sometimes it is because of a view that funding will be cheaper, or assets will produce higher returns, if the transaction is delayed.

It should no longer be that the corporate FD simply hasn't a clue, or abdicates the decision. The literature produced on Risk Management and derivatives, especially since Barings, for treasurers, directors and FDs alike, can leave no one in any doubt what it is all about (*The Role of the Finance Director*, FT Pitman, 2nd edition 1998).

Volatile interest rates, reflected by random changes in the level and shape of the yield curve, expose corporates to substantial and growing interest rate risk. Admittedly, before and during the advent of swaps, it was often not possible to exactly hedge interest rate risk for intermediate periods between normal market periods, i.e. 1, 2, 3, 6, 9, 12 months, etc. However, now there is little excuse, as term and basis can usually be accommodated by swaps alone or in conjunction with, e.g. FRAs, for most periods out to five years or more.

There is a wide and growing methodology for measuring, managing and evaluating interest rate risk, which is beyond the scope of this book. Suffice to say, that a term liability, funding a term asset, on a mismatched basis, while capable of being matched through the use of swaps, does not stand in isolation in the corporation's balance sheet, nor in the overall interest rate (and indeed currency) profile of risk.

Interest rate swaps - evolving through need, maturing as opportunities

Corporates and financial institutions alike need the ability to structure their interest rate assets and liabilities to produce the optimum overall return at a managed level of risk and to be able to flex this to take account of changes in the yield curve and still sustain the optimum return.

The original value of swaps was in enabling especially those with good credit ratings, or with differential ratings or credit assessments between one market or one group of lenders and another, to take advantage of the 'arbitrages' to effect cheapest funding. The original role of banks was as intermediates between counterparties, often seeking out the counterparty with the matching stream of interest rates desired (e.g. fixed rate term, versus LIBOR related floating), to effect the swap and take a fee out of the arbitrage in between.

As the volumes grew, the banks increasingly became temporary counterparties until another could be found. Then they became counterparties themselves. And finally became investors and traders with a portfolio of derivatives as part of their revenue streams, as well as holistic interest rate and balance sheet risk management. With the growing sophistication of the analysts and treasurers, they invented and manufactured new generations of synthetic products, sometimes to meet increasingly esoteric needs and at others, to create new marketing, trading and revenue opportunities. The range of mortgage products owes its source to derivatives used to create and manage the risk.

Nowadays, 80 per cent or more of bond and similar issues are swapped on behalf of issuers into other currency and interest rate bases. It is also not unusual for swaps to be created to reverse previous transactions, due to changes in the corporate interest rate profile, or even market structures and yield curves. The international capital markets are usually rich in needs and opportunities. Credit ratings and country risks are constantly changing, with the result that interest rate swap spreads can fluctuate widely for different issuers, different countries and in the market as a whole. After Russia's problems in 1998, spreads widened dramatically and the Latin American and Far-Eastern troubles hardly helped!

Both corporates and banks can be differently rated in different countries. For example, there are domestic rating agencies in each of the UK, USA and Japan. Although Moodies and Standard & Poors remain globally prevalent, they do not rate all companies and there are different ratings for different types of liabilities. Depending on the view the corporate treasurer wishes to take, this can produce all sorts of anomalies and therefore swap opportunities. This is also true between bank borrowings and capital debt. The Halifax Bank and Imperial Chemical Industries (ICI) may be able to borrow at similar rates for three-months, but the Halifax will raise funds much closer to the equivalent Government Bond for 5-10 years. With its corporate treasury now a profit centre and needing short-term investments all the time, Halifax could take either an investment or a swap view which leads to both them and ICI being satisfied.

Liquidity in different markets can also drive the need for swaps. Sometimes this liquidity can be name or sector driven. During the 'gold rush' of swaps driven medium term funding in the late 1980s, the building societies managed to close one or two markets against themselves by saturating them with issues. They simply moved on to other markets and swapped the consequent currency and interest rate risks as necessary to produce the desired funding, risk and duration profiles they wanted.

Swaps developed from various anomalies such as these. The result is that nowadays, not very good names can issue and swap 'junk bonds' in all sorts of markets to raise funds at terms that they otherwise might not achieve. The bond can be passed to investors at an attractive enough rate or, using an array of derivatives, 'stripped' and chopped up. This will produce short-term, zero coupon, deep discounted, etc investments to suit end users' desired tax, accounting and cashflow profiles, or even to match their own interest rate exposures.

What they are

We have defined interest rate swaps briefly and the mechanics, maths and technicalities of how they work elsewhere. In essence, they are agreements by which two parties agree to pay each other interest on a notional amount over an agreed period, calculated according to different interest rate bases. Originally and in the most simple example, one party wanted fixed rate liabilities but had a better credit standing in short-term markets, while the other wanted variable rate liabilities and had a better longer term credit profile than the short-term counterparty. The first would borrow or issue an echelon of short-term liabilities, the latter would issue medium term debt and the two simply agreed to exchange each others' interest streams at agreed rates which provided a gain to both. If a bank had to act as intermediator or arranger, they charged a fee out of the arbitrage in the middle.

Many other swaps have evolved, including the 'floating-floating' swap, for different basis periods. Other more esoteric variants are discussed later. It should be borne in mind that the principal amounts are merely notional and therefore usually regarded as 'off-balance sheet', as no funds are lent or borrowed between the parties. For simplicity sake, when payment dates coincide, interest payments are netted between the two parties. Where a fixed or floating rate to zero coupon swap is effected, the payment of, e.g. periodic floating rate payments and a single counter payment at the end of the term, would presumably suit the respective parties' cashflow, tax and accounting regimes.

Swaps can now readily be effected for sums of £500,000 or more, for terms which may extend out to 25 years. The norm would usually be £5-10 million, for 2 to 10 years. Swap spreads have proved to be volatile, as described earlier. Originally, they were priced between counterparties, or by a banking intermediary, usually to give both parties an equivalent gain, after the banker's 'fee'. Now, they are usually priced off short-dated interest rate futures. The whole interest rate and derivatives market is now driven by highly sophisticated computerised mathematical models, such as Black-Scholes, the Capital Asset Pricing Model, Betas, Multiple Factor Interest Rate Risk models, etc, building on the original thoughts of Markowitz, Modigliani and Miller, together with Monte Carlo and Portfolio theories.

Swap spreads

Swap spreads can be defined as the difference between swap rates and the underlying benchmark bond yields for the fixed rate period. With the maturity of the market, the margin from bid to offer can be as little as two or three basis points. Spreads themselves started at 100bp (basis points) or more in the early 1980s and had traded broadly between 10-50bp until

August 1998. High spreads reflect poor liquidity in the market. In the early days, this was because deals had to be matched. More recently it was because of turbulence in world markets.

As markets have become more sophisticated, derivatives have become 'productised' and portfolios are traded round the clock. Swap spreads may vary from hour to hour. While it is common to take positions in interest rates using absolute or derived instruments (such as swaps), it is also more common for traders to take a position on swap spreads alone.

Swap spreads are important because they can drive the appetite for bond issues alone. With a huge proportion of such issues now being done in order to produce swapped funds, rather than as issues in themselves, it could truly be said that 'the tail is wagging the dog'.

Swap spreads are driven by supply and demand, in and between markets. When there is market uncertainty, more issuers will want to secure a fixed rate, to hedge against rising interest rates. With an excess demand by fixed rate payers, in a market reluctant to buy fixed rate bonds, due to their own concerns about rising interest rates, spreads must widen. Demand for short dated variable investments will increase until the uncertainty passes and demand for medium term fixed rate bonds must decline, as investors are reluctant to lock into fixed returns against rising markets. This will mirror the likely needs of borrowers. Seeking to lock in cost of funds in case rates rise, they will wish to swap away floating rate payments and be willing to pay a fixed rate stream, until the storm abates.

In the light of the 1998 devaluation of the rouble, swap spreads soared. In mid-August the 5 year swap spread was 57bp (basis points) and the 15 years spread 39bp. By early afternoon on 25 August, these had widened to 108bp and 94bp respectively. At the beginning of September, they had still only returned to 82bp and 78bp respectively.

The market convention for quoting USD (US dollar) swaps is to quote the all-in cost of the fixed part versus the opposite floating part. The all-in-cost (equivalent to the internal rate of return, or IRR) is expressed either as an absolute semi-annual interest level, or, as discussed above as a basis point spread to the semi-annual bond equivalent of, e.g. the US Treasury yield curve.

While notionally it is a spread against the underlying government bond or security (gilt in the UK), there are not such bonds in issue for every possible maturity date for the next 15 years. As swap business is being executed minute by minute, let alone daily, the swap is priced against a notional bond yield interpolated between actual yields of bonds in issue, from e.g. the T-bond yield curve. The market convention for pricing UK swaps is equivalent, priced off Gilts.

To summarise, the main drivers of swap spreads are:
● Credit;
● Bond issues;
● The demand for asset and liability hedges;
● Supply and demand factors for the underlying government securities or bond issues.

As the bond issues, which create the fixed side of the swap, are non-government (and often bank issues), spreads can reflect the market's perception of bank risk against government security risk at a given point in time.

Bond issuers drive swap spreads, through the demand for receipt of the fixed rate, tending to narrow spreads accordingly. On the other hand, liability hedgers and asset swaps will tend to drive out the spreads - payers of the fixed widen the spread and investors paying fixed on the swap will arbitrage unusually tight spreads.

As the fixed side is priced against government securities, it follows that a relative scarcity of such securities can have the same impact as an excess of swaps driven bond issues. Equally, anomalies in the volume of issues for particular terms of either, can cause 'bumps' in the yield curve and therefore swap spreads for the same term, until these are arbitraged out or smoothed out by bond issues for terms around the anomalous maturity.

With the whole world trading on a semi-virtual basis through screens, driven by computer based mathematical models of prices and yield curves, the opportunities for arbitrage seen 20 years ago must seem like a dream now.

Chapter 5

Currency Swaps

Very few companies are unaffected by currency risk, whether directly or indirectly. Even if a company has no sales in overseas markets, its domestic demand can be affected by currency changes, such that, say, a rise in the value of sterling makes import costs relatively cheaper and overseas producers or suppliers may find it more financially attractive to sell into sterling markets.

Foreign Exchange Management

Most companies buy from abroad, whether it be raw materials, energy, finished goods or capital equipment. Furthermore, even finished or part-manufactured goods (including components) may often have an overseas input at some stage of the manufacturing or assembly process. Again, changes in currencies could make it more attractive to source from abroad, in today's global markets.

For any company with direct foreign currency exposures, either as buyer or seller, the need for a sophisticated understanding of currency management has existed for some considerable time. There are three very simple strategies that an exposed organisation could adopt: do nothing (passive, and by definition, speculative); hedge everything that moves (expensive, time consuming and maybe ultimately self-defeating); or rational, informed risk management, based on awareness, understanding, evaluation, analysis and optimal decisions.

Types of Exposure

We have talked elsewhere of economic, transaction and translation exposure. To these can be added strategic and pre-transactional exposure. The former is where there is an explicit or implicit foreign exchange risk related to competitors' strategic decisions. The latter is related to the decisions which take place before a transaction is implemented, such as issuing a price list to customers, submitting tenders, or capital equipment purchasing decisions (often involving substantial currency settlements) before the purchase itself is implemented.

The principle of risk management is that management should understand and anticipate risks, taking decisions accordingly. Sound strategic management will include a consideration of strategic currency risks and their possible effect on net worth. For pre-transactional exposures, the key point may well be how far in advance to take a view. For the other exposures, a mature risk management process as discussed earlier, should pick up and handle the risks accordingly.

When we talk about speculation, we may consider strategic or tactical speculation. Strategic could be 'betting the company'. Some Japanese companies set up subsidiaries specifically for speculating in derivatives, to enhance earnings. One chemical company failed spectacularly when failed speculation wiped out the net worth of its core business. Even tactical speculation can be dangerous. Nick Leeson wiped out Barings by exceeding his authority in Japanese equity derivatives.

It must be understood, however, that you cannot run a business successfully without, by definition, speculating. If you eliminate all risk, you may not only eliminate all profit opportunities, but you could in theory end up with net losses, due to the fee cost of the hedges used. Let's assume that most companies and all banks recognise and want to make money by trading in markets which involve direct or indirect currency risks.

For transactional risks, the choice may lie between: netting intra company currency exposures within and across the company, group or bank; understanding and conscious acceptance of a certain level of risk (without undue or outright speculation); hedging through such as foreign currency swaps. Translation exposures will always affect the balance sheet, either directly in terms of the net worth of assets minus liabilities, or indirectly through the profit and loss account. Possible responses include: maintaining constant currency gearing in each currency (so that the effect may be consistently proportionate); maintaining consistent interest cover in each currency; hedging net overseas earnings, beyond those remitted back into the domestic currency; hedging overseas subsidiary balance sheets in local currencies or through swaps.

Swaps are only one of the possible hedging instruments. The others include: simple borrowing and lending; forwards and futures; options; swaptions; and other derivative or synthetic structures.

A bank or corporate's foreign exchange exposure, or foreign exchange position, is the net difference between both 'in-value' and not-in-value assets and liabilities in a particular currency. The total equivalent outright exposure across all currencies could only be aggregated by translating into one benchmark currency, such as sterling or dollars, but normally the base or home currency. Where total currency assets exceed liabilities, the company is said to be long, or hold a long position. When liabilities exceed assets they are short. In the unlikely event they are equal, the book is 'square'. Of course, in the home currency, a long foreign exchange exposure would be short and vice-versa. In the case of a bank, the aggregate position would include elements for trading, hedging and internal management purposes and might be viewed separately for such purposes.

Foreign Exchange practices

Before getting into the specifics of currency swaps, it is important to identify some concepts and market practices, relating to: value dates; rates; spot and forward positions; regulation and best practice.

Value dates

Foreign exchange includes both cash and forward transactions, but the established practice is for a 'cash' transaction to be dealt 'spot', i.e. two business days after the deal date. In this case, the 'spot' date is the value date (i.e. the date on which value passes). The date on which the deal is agreed between the parties is known as the deal date. It is possible to deal for value the same day ('same day rate') or for one day forward ('one day rate' or 'tom-next'). Both of these latter are effectively short-dated forward deals. Together with forward rates, they are all varying functions of the spot rate and calculated off it.

Forward Exchange positions

While the bank or corporate may maintain a 'square' foreign exchange book of aggregated in-value and not-in-value deals, the forward maturity ladder of not-in-value deals must be carefully monitored, as they are unlikely to match out day to day and therefore there may be individual short or long positions to settle as the ladder moves forward. Each is an individual foreign exchange and interest rate risk (as each deal matures, it will have to be funded or utilise currency deposits or currency swaps at what may be varying rates of interest).

Forex rates

While in common parlance one may talk of buying and selling commodities or other financial instruments, it should be remembered that each foreign exchange transaction implies both a buy and sell order. Buying dollars from London involves selling sterling contemporaneously, unless another currency is being exchanged.

Market practice since 1944 means that currencies are normally quoted in terms of their dollar rate and rates between other currencies tend to be calculated as cross-rates, i.e. the sterling/ drachma rate can be derived from the sterling/dollar rate and the dollar/drachma rate. You may note that the prime exception is sterling dollar, due to the former pre-eminence of sterling. Commonly, therefore, sterling/dollar is quoted as the number of dollars to one pound sterling, as opposed to the number of French francs to the dollar. This has also tended to be true of some of the former 'Scheduled Territories' (e.g. Australia and New Zealand).

The main influences on foreign exchange rates used to be balance of payments and capital flows, but now, with 95+% of all forex transactions being for speculative purposes, it is global capital flows which cause volatility in currency rates. The Bank of England has continued to manage sterling to try and achieve stability, within certain parameters and, by and large has succeeded to keep it fairly stable against a weighted basket of currencies, with the notable exception of when the pound was attacked during its brief membership of the EMS.

Spot rates

Cash rates are quoted in terms of spot, with a spread (not a swap spread) between bid and offer, to remunerate the market maker. They are normally relatively small, even as low as one or two basis points (bp). The market quotes have become by practice truncated, also. So, if the price of sterling was $1.6075-80, the dealer would quote it as '75-80', relying on the awareness and honesty of the prospective buyer or seller to know the 'big figure'.

Forward rates

A foreign exchange contract is an agreement to buy or sell a specific currency on a specified future date, or during a specified period, at a rate agreed on the deal date. Although at any one time there may be a huge outstanding demand for forward foreign exchange, there is no trade in forward foreign exchange. Instead, the trading is done in swap prices, quoted in basis points. A forex swap is a purchase of one currency and simultaneous sale of another currency for spot delivery and an opposite sale of the first currency and simultaneous purchase of the other currency for value on an agreed future date. There are also bid and offered sides to swap prices, but fluctuation tends between a range, established by interest rate differentials between the two currencies. Outside of this range, there are arbitrage opportunities in the deposit swaps.

The forward swap price involves a consideration of these same deposit rates, because the purchaser assumes the need to borrow funds in the said currency to settle the future payment, while the funds generated can be lent in the relevant currency until required to meet future obligations. These complexities are factored into the swap calculations analysed elsewhere.

London Code of Conduct

In July 1995, the Bank of England issued the London Code, whose main aim was "to set out in a clear and concise manner the principles and standards which broking firms and their employees, and 'core principals' in the wholesale markets....and their employees should observe."

The products covered include: sterling wholesale deposits; foreign currency wholesale deposits; spot and forward foreign exchange; many other financial debt instruments; and interest rate and currency swaps, regardless of their original maturity...together with many derivatives, bullion and gilt repos.

The Code's main elements relate to General Standards for principals and brokers; Controls; Dealing Principles and Procedures: A Statement of Best Practice; Market Conventions; Guidelines For Exchanging Standard Settlement Instructions; and a Market Notice on dual broking arrangements in relation to Foreign Exchange Dealing.

BBAIRS and ISDA

In 1985, the British Bankers' Association published *Recommended Terms and Conditions* for interest rate and currency swaps (BBAIRS) to standardise practice for price quotations, negotiations and documentation for swaps in London. Nowadays, most swaps are written under ISDA standard terms (International Swaps Dealers Association, Inc., New York).

These include standard Definitions and an ISDA Master Agreement. The latter covers payments, representations, events of default, early termination, transfer, contractual currencies, notices, law and definition of terms used within an agreement.

Currency Swaps

In a currency swap, the parties exchange cash flows in one currency for cash flows in another, more or less equivalent to a deposit in one currency and a matched borrowing in another. In practice, they agree to buy specific amounts of foreign currency from each other at spot and sell the same amounts for delivery on an agreed future value date. The fixed rate of exchange is established at the commencement and used as the basis for the payment flows throughout the deal, including principal at commencement, principal at the end of the swap and any interest payments on the currency that each party may have to make periodically throughout the deal (depending on the term and intervening periods).

The basis of interest payments may be agreed as: fixed-fixed; floating-floating; or fixed-floating, as between the two currencies. While exchange of currencies at commencement is o ptional if based on current market rates, exchange of principal takes place at maturity; and interest payments for intervening periods are paid gross without netting.

Currency swaps are obviously more complex and more risky than interest swaps, as they involve both currency exchange and interest rate deposits. While currency swaps may be for larger amounts than interest rate swaps, they may be for shorter terms (i.e. up to 10 years as opposed to 15).

Banks will not now usually seek a counterparty for a swap, often simply adding them to their swaps and derivatives portfolio. Indeed the sophistication of such portfolios is now such that transactions may be fitted into the overall duration and yield curve related profile, or matched out with a complex mixture of various derivatives and deposits.

Management, valuation and evaluation of swaps books is essentially based on the principle of discounted cash flow, as being the simplest way to bring everything to a common standard of measurement. Any fixed rate payment profile will be known at the outset, because the currency rate is fixed for the term of the deal and so is the interest rate.

The floating rate profile can be calculated against market indexes every three, six or whatever months. At each such reset, the expected cashflows can be reduced to present value, alongside the known fixed rate cashflows, allowing the sensitivity to market rates or the yield curve to be calculated at any time.

Matching out the risks, using a mix of other instruments or other deals in the book and marking to market for accounting purposes (including setting aside funds against possible losses) represents good practice. The corporate treasury position may be less sophisticated than this, but essentially the same good practice is recommended, especially on a PVBP (present value for book purposes), weighted duration basis.

Chapter 6

Esoteric Swaps

From humble beginnings only around 20 years ago, (the first currency swap is reckoned to have been between IBM and the World Bank in 1981) swaps business has exploded in growth and helped fuel the global prosperity of the late 20th century (and the consequent volatility of markets). Following the development of swaps, a raft of derivatives has evolved, together with countless synthesised products.

The swaps markets themselves have evolved to match corporate needs. From the early liability swaps allowing two counterparties to exchange fixed for floating rate interest payment streams and currency swaps, which enhanced the ability to raise money through international fixed rate bond markets and convert the proceeds back into LIBOR related floating rate domestic currency commitments, many variants have been developed to meet the needs of the corporate treasurer.

In this section, we shall cover: swaptions; forward swaps; total return swaps; equity swaps; asset swaps; SONIAs; credit, credit-linked and credit-default swaps; yield curve lock swaps; tax rate swaps; and property swaps.

Swaptions

Since their invention in the mid 1980s, swaptions have exploded in growth. A swaption is simply an option on a swap. They fall into two types (receiver or payer), with two options (call or put) and two decisions (buy or sell). A call is an option to contract, or 'buy' a swap within a given fixed period. A put is the opposite of a call and effectively confers the opportunity to 'sell' an option. Each buyer of a call needs a corresponding seller, but this does not necessarily result in a put.

A receiver option gives the buyer the right with no obligation to receive the stream of fixed rate payments in a swap which, if it were to correspond with an original payer swap (i.e. pay the fixed rate) would enable the unwinding of the commitment leaving a floating rate liability. A swaption can be bought or sold.

With debt markets containing treasurers and book managers wanting cheap, flexible hedges, investors looking for better yields without higher credit risks, issuers wanting better more flexible terms and speculators living off the proceeds, the evolution of the swaption market was in many ways as important as the development of other derivatives. Other structures which evolved from swaptions were: revisable swaps, range cancellable swaps; ratchet swaps; and double-up swaps. In the first, the borrower buys a receiver swaption and then sells one at a lower strike rate, allowing them to lock in a lower fixed rate if rates fall.

A range cancellable swap conferred the right on the payer to cancel a swap at a specific date if the residual fixed rate fell within a predetermined range. The ratchet swap allows the borrower to pay a lower fixed rate initially by stating whether the fixed rate of a future swap will be above or below a given strike rate. The double-up swap is also derived from a forward receiver swap, where by giving the bank the right to double up the notional amount at the start date, the investor can increase the fixed return on a receiving swap.

Forward Swaps

A forward swap is an interest rate swap with a forward start. This enables the possibility of locking into fixed rates at the present levels without any swap accruals taking place until some future date. Forward swaps are most attractive when the yield curve is flat or inverse (downward sloping), and no premium will be charged for the delayed start.

The most common use of a forward swap has been for the purpose of extending the maturity of an existing swap, where the fixed rate payer wishes to take advantage of lower interest rates. They may also be used to lock in a fixed rate before maturity of the existing borrowings, thus avoiding the need for prefinancing on a fixed rate basis.

Credit risk of swaps and credit-related swaps

While we are not dealing with the credit risk associated with swaps here, a brief discussion is relevant. We have reviewed different types of risk elsewhere and the most obvious risk related to swaps is the counterparty risk. This, in itself, has diminished substantially since the appearance of swaps, now that banks are so often the counterparty.

The credit risk associated with derivatives is much more complex than that of cash-based instruments, because it is substantially market-related. Leaving aside the counterparty risk, there will be a high degree of correlation between the degree of credit risk and the amount by which the underlying interest rate or currency has moved since the derivative transaction was entered into (although this movement can be adverse or beneficial).

The credit risk inherent in swaps (and other derivatives) can be subdivided into full value risk and market risk. The former results from the non-simultaneous exchange of assets, especially spot currency transactions, deposits, non-collateralised investments and traded securities where settlement isn't on the basis of payment on delivery. Market risk is the value of the loss which would occur due to a change in the terms of the underlying asset, in the event that the counterparty defaulted. These would include both interest rate and currency swaps.

In essence, the credit risk of a swap can be captured in the replacement cost of the swap, at the time of default. However, to be even more prudent, one would add an allowance for future adverse interest rate or currency movements, noting that, where there are periodic payments and resets, the profile of credit risk is stepped, not smooth.

To complicate matters further, where there are a number of credit exposures to a particular counterparty, by virtue of a number of swaps for different maturities, or even of a different nature, being outstanding with a particular counterparty, the credit risk can be subdivided further. There may be a total risk of default, or the defaulter may arbitrarily 'cherry-pick' the risk (i.e. settle or close the most advantageous swaps, before general default).

The Hammmersmith & Fulham debacle and what followed, once it was seen that swaps were *ultra vires* for local authorities, led to much greater focus on the credit risks inherent in the legal documentation itself. In particular, there may be certain defined 'events of default': failure to make payments when due; misrepresentation; default under the swaps specified in the agreement; cross default; bankruptcy;

etc. The wider significance of documentation is such that where there is a common counterparty to several swaps, default on one will automatically trigger default or repudiation of all the others.

The techniques for reducing such risk include netting and off-setting of mutual obligations between counterparties (which has become included in standard documentation), termination clauses linked to ratings downgrades, etc.

In relation to the credit risk related to swaps or credit risk in general, there is no substitute for detailed appraisal and awareness of risks, constant, ongoing evaluation of the movement of such risks and a spread portfolio approach. This is applicable to the balance sheet and profit and loss account as a whole but the swaps market has evolved to allow for the swapping (and indeed the general hedging) of credit and credit-related risks.

Credit-related swaps

There are three main types of credit derivatives: the credit-linked or credit-default swap; derivatives based on credit spreads; and total return credit swaps (or total return swap, dealt with below).

The credit-linked or credit default swap are activated in the event of a credit default. This could be anything which impacts either the creditworthiness or the credit rating of the issuer or counterparty, e.g. corporate, sovereign state, government body, bank or other financial institution, etc.

Banks and financial institutions have become highly sophisticated in managing or hedging credit risk, whereas for corporates credit risk is a daily exposure in the ordinary course of commercial operation. The latter are not in the business of risk management or derivatives origination or trading, however. The aspects and tools of debt management have evolved to deal with credit risk to a certain extent, with such as factoring, but mature companies, while ostensibly being exposed to standard payment terms (e.g. 7, 30, 90 days - where these are adhered to!), are actually exposed to a revolving and regular credit risk from their regular trading partners (i.e. customers).

Whereas financial institutions can readily manage their credit risk by selling, syndicating, spreading or otherwise reducing the risk, non-financial companies have different types of investment or asset. While all companies are owed money, with the corporate it is a debtor. With the financial institution, it may well be a loan or similar financial instrument. As well as factoring, corporates can also consider credit insurance, through an insurance policy.

Unfortunately, while insurers themselves are becoming more adept at the use of derivatives for underwriting their own exposures and are now even writing derivatives insurance, their familiarity and cover is more sporadic than the market as a whole. Furthermore, insurance companies often cherry pick their risks, either directly, by declining to insure or limiting the cover of, certain types of risk, or scarcity pricing the cover to discourage such risks.

The credit default swap is a market driven instrument. It is activated on the incidence of bankruptcy or insolvency, ratings agency downgrade, debt default or previously specified price declines in an underlying or reference security, or basket of such securities. It can provide protection for as long as is required (provided the price asked by the writer of the risk is acceptable to the riskholder).

In its simplest form it is activated by the simple default of another debtor company. It is an OTC instrument, substantiated usually by standard ISDA based documentation. The credit swap will be based on an agreed and appropriate reference asset, basket of assets or index, which should ideally be publicly traded and having a high correlation to the underlying receivables. Once the trigger event has been agreed upon, the bank which is accepting the risk can calculate the cost of the swap, which will once again normally be structured as a stream of quarterly payments throughout the life of the asset.

(For this purpose, it would be useful to think of rolling credit as essentially a quasi-permanent rolling 90 day instrument (where that is the due period of the receivables), more or less equivalent to a three-month LIBOR linked instrument. It is not fixed rate by nature, as interest rates vary daily throughout the term). If there is default at any time, the bank pays the Creditor Company an amount calculated in relation to the reference asset(s).

The credit swap may be used by a financial institution:
- ✔ to reduce exposure to a deteriorating credit;
- ✔ to free up credit lines;
- ✔ to protect against downgrading of a specific credit risk;
- ✔ to reduce credit exposures which have exceeded limits as a result of adverse movements in interest rates and/ or currency movements; etc.

Financial institutions would also be most likely to benefit from the use of derivatives based on credit spreads. Here, swaps and other derivatives structured around the spread between a bond (e.g. corporate bond) and an appropriate government security can be used as a way to isolate the credit risk on a credit sensitive debt. There have, for example, been cases where the breach of a given spread level has triggered the right to swap from one security into another, or a specified group of securities.

Total return swap

Total rate of return (TROR) swaps transfer the whole economic performance of a reference asset or index, including all associated cash flows, including appreciation or depreciation (i.e., marking to market, in the case of quoted securities). They are one of the most prevalent forms of credit related derivative. With investors constantly seeking ways to improve the overall return on investments, the TROR swap offers just such a means to earn a higher total yield.

Investors or corporates may not have the means to determine the credit worthiness of investments or issuers. Accordingly, the end effect of a TROR can be to transfer the whole of the credit risk to a bank, in return for receiving, say LIBOR related payments secured on the bank's own name as a counterparty. This would be especially attractive where either the investor did not wish to, was precluded from, or was unable to (due to illiquidity or an uneconomic price) realise an investment.

In the simplest case of a total return swap, between two banks, one pays to the other all the stream of fixed rate periodical payments, together with the positive mark-to-market move-ments in the value of the underlying bond. The second bank pays the stream of all the periodical LIBOR related payments, plus the negative mark-to-market movements in the underlying bond. The net effect of this is that the total performance of the bond has been transferred from the first bank to the second, whether the first bank holds the relevant bond or not. Notwith-standing this, each has, of course, acquired a counterparty ex-posure to the other.

Equity swaps

Forwards, futures, puts and calls on equity effectively originated well before the 1980s. It was inevitable, there-fore, with the growth of the swap market, that equity swaps would develop.

Whether as a trade or investment holder, many situations arise where the holder of an equity stake wishes to get rid of the economic risk inherent in holding that stake, but can wait for a more propitious time to sell the stake itself (e.g. for market liquidity reasons). Of course, options and fu-tures provide many appropriate opportunities for the largest quoted stocks, but matters become much more complex for smaller or unquoted companies.

Although the frequency and visibility of equity swaps may be far less than interest or currency equivalents, the circumstances in which they are used can make them just as economically significant. We are again, here, getting into the field of asset/liability management and hedging the holistic value of the balance sheet (back to net worth and value at risk).

Normally, OTC equity derivatives are based on either an option contract or equity swap. The key determinants may well be the legal and accounting treatment of different structures or even regulation or management policy.

As for the total return swap, in the case of an equity swap the holder of the equity is passing the performance of the equity stake to a bank, in return for a stream of LIBOR related payments, having also built in the mark-to-market changes as appropriate. The result is that although the investment remains on balance sheet, its risk has been converted into that of a short dated LIBOR related instrument (together with the acquired counterparty risks of course). Thus the holder is immunised from price risk, but also loses potential capital appreciation and dividends. In some cases, the swap is made against the characteristics of another security (e.g. bond), rather than LIBOR.

Equity swaps can be particularly useful for overseas denominated securities, either as a way to gain access to a market without the underlying risks, or as a means to hedge the currency and other associated risks of an overseas market. They can be as esoteric as the two parties wish, e.g. related to a high liquidity security, a basket of investments, or even the whole index in a particular market. For overseas investments, the characteristics of the equity and a currency swap can be combined.

Asset swaps

Historically, interest rate and currency swaps developed rapidly, as companies have relatively large and ongoing needs to fund their short, medium and long-term capital requirements. Where they have investments, these are more likely to be diverse, varying in size and relatively small scale by comparison with borrowings. As will be seen later, with the discussion of total balance sheet management. Corporate treasurers prefer certainty and, in a perfectly safe world, would match all asset and liability characteristics of the balance sheet, in order to have certainty of return. Where there are diverse investments held, this was more problematical before the evolution of the asset swap.

Not dissimilar from the equity or total return swap in nature, they can be used either to hedge out, or change the nature or basis of the risks inherent in a particular investment, or to change the characteristics of one investment in the balance sheet (e.g. a bond), into those of a desired type of investment (e.g., an equity). Taking the liability and asset swaps together, their potential is to enhance the ability to manage the balance sheet holistically, on a portfolio basis.

While asset swaps were slow to develop for companies and investors, they began to be rapidly seen as another attractive revenue stream possibility for banks in their own investment or trading portfolios. Banks do not make any money unless they take on risk. And, while risk is inherent in the commercial operations of any corporate, they exist for the prime purpose of making or selling products or services, not trading esoteric, high risk derivatives (although this has not stopped some losing sight of this purpose to great expense as we shall see later).

To put it simply therefore, an asset swap is a structure that enables an investor or holder of a particular asset to change the nature and timing of the inherent risk into a different, desired set of characteristics. So, a holder of an unquoted equity may be able to change the holistic capital and dividend risk into a stream of fixed rate payments, equivalent to a medium term bond. The holder of a fixed interest rate security may wish to change the nature of the cashflows to that of a series of other-currency denominated LIBOR-related receipts, to match out a similar foreign currency denominated liability, etc.

SONIAS

In the 1970s particularly, especially during and after the successive oil crises, interest rates were highly volatile. In 1977, the sterling overnight rate was recorded at 450% on one particular day, as a North American bank found itself short just before the markets closed.

After Britain's shadow entry into EMU and the attack on the currency by speculators in the early 1990s, short-term interest rates were put up by 5% in one day. Due almost entirely to liquidity considerations, together with interest rate expectations, the overnight rate, while being much more stable than the above examples, can be quite volatile at times.

It would not be surprising to think of swaps in terms of longer term considerations, at the very least from three-months out, but in the last few years, SONIAS (or overnight indexed swaps) have evolved. The point is that all short-term derivatives are valued and settle on expectations of interest rates over the relevant term (characteristically three-months).

Implicit in that assumption is that daily rates (i.e. overnight rates) will accord with the shape of the predicted yield curve at the outset. This can be a long way from what happens in practice. So, what are the consequences and how have SONIAS evolved?

It is perfectly possible for the daily fixing of reference rates for LIBOR related instruments or their derivatives to diverge from one day to the next, irrespective of official pronouncements on rates, purely because of the balance of market views on the future of interest rates. In the 1980s, for example, when interest rate changes were triggered by the demand for Treasury Bills on a Thursday, market forces had a much greater effect on interest rate changes. Even now, however, on the day before or the day of the Bank of England's announcement on rates, expectations can be variable.

In 1997, SONIA (sterling overnight index average) first made an appearance and SONIAS (or OIS, overnight indexed swaps) soon followed. Portfolios of fixing-based instruments are much more volatile than portfolios of the equivalent underlying cash based instruments. At first, this problem was addressed by introducing more frequent fixings, shorter gaps and more complex products, which helped to close the risk gap between the two. Eventually, SONIAS (SONIA swaps, or OIS), developed, which used SONIA as a floating rate itself.

So, the OIS is a fixed/floating rate swap, tied to a daily overnight or Tom/next rate. The term can range from one week to one year, with benchmarks at 1, 2, 3, 4, 5, 6, 9 and 12 months. The two parties exchange at maturity the difference between the fixed rate stream of payments and the floating rate stream based on SONIA.

The effect is that an OIS acts as a cash instrument over the period. They enhance the management of non-fixing related portfolios and allow the investor or borrower to achieve actual interest rates, rather than a constantly moving set of expectations (where periodic fixings are exposed

to changing interest rates, changing interest rate expectations and the consequent changing shape of the yield curve.)

Yield curve lock swaps

We shall talk later about yield curves. Following the dramatic
increase in both the levels of volatility and interest rates themselves in the 1970s, the yield curve started to change shape.
Traditionally, the normal yield curve is upward sloping
throughout its length, tapering down towards parallel at the
future end. Particularly since the early 1980s, we have had an
inverse or even downward sloping curve.

This implies an expectation that in the longer term, rates will
be lower than at present. The yield curve is predicated on bond
yields and investors who buy the fixed returns on medium and
long dated government securities to secure them while they
can, cause the flattening.

Volatility has caused changing shapes, while actual interest
rate changes change the pitch of the slope at the short end.
These two factors can cause both the fixed and floating payer
to scratch their heads. The floating payer will see the yield
curve predicting the likely levels of future fixings. The fixed
payer may look at the longer, inverted end of a yield curve and
wonder whether they wish to remain locked into the present
level of fixed payments if the curve is predicting a down turn
further out.

Both will, by definition, be taking a view on the overall level
of rates, by virtue of their respective positions. Presumably the
fixed payer believes rates will not fall overall and the variable
payer either anticipates falls, or takes the view that the total

present value of the stream of payments will be lower than the outturn on the present value of the fixed payments.

A yield curve lock swap allows the fixed rate paying borrower to enter into a long-term swap at a predetermined spread over a future LIBOR index, at any stage up to a given date. This protects the borrower against a steepening yield curve (i.e. relatively stable short-term rates, but rising longer term fixed rates).

Tax rate swaps

In summer 1994, Morgan Grenfell created the first known tax rate swap. This has led to some evolution of a market for tax rate protection. The idea is to bring together potential counterparties, one of which will benefit if tax rates rise and the other if they fall. Not surprisingly, HM Treasurer was not tempted into receiving the swap of lower tax rates, but one counterparty was found who was able to create an advantage and the swap was done.

A tax rate swap works in essence like this: it is equivalent to an interest rate swap. The difference is that one party elects to pay the equivalent of a preset, fixed rate of tax on a notional amount of profit and the other party elects to pay the actual (i.e. floating) rate of tax on the same notional amount. There is no effect on the actual amount of tax paid to the Inland Revenue.

The example is quoted here for two reasons. First, it is an example of the extraordinary and growing ingenuity in the swaps market in particular and derivatives in general. Second, it provokes the thought of swapping the equivalent of tax liabilities across international boundaries.

Property Swaps

The final esoteric example quoted here is the property swap (we have only scratched the surface really - if you have any position you want to hedge or manage, just ask an appropriate trading bank whether they can manufacture the appropriate product to meet your needs.

When we review balance sheet management later, you will see the value of being able to hedge or change the nature and characteristics of any asset or liability in the balance sheet. Property, by virtue of usually being regarded as the longest term asset, tends to be regarded as a fixed rate asset. In a perfect world, it would be matched by an appropriate fixed rate liability of an equivalent term (e.g. 25-100 years!).

In March 1997, Graham Sargen wrote an excellent article in The Treasurer, about the development of Property Index Forwards. Now, these aren't swaps. However, if an equity swap or total return swap can be constructed around exchanging the future income stream plus net mark to market gains, for a LIBOR related stream, the same can be done for property.

Whether the term desired would prove a sticking point, is moot, but with the term of swaps extending steadily and the liquidity and creativity of the markets expanding, it must now be possible to swap the characteristics of any asset or liability in a corporate or banking balance sheet. When augmented by the panoply of other derivatives, duration based total balance sheet management (see later), becomes a practical possibility.

Conclusion

The purpose of this chapter, following the foregoing ones on interest rate and currency swaps, is to illustrate that swaps have evolved to the stage where even without the use of other derivatives, an extraordinary range of risks can be accepted, managed or hedged, through the use of swaps alone. When the array of other derivatives, including commodity futures, etc, is added to the consideration, it can be seen that almost any financial risk and balance sheet can be hedged wholly or to some degree of correlation. That is provided a counterparty or trader can be found to take the other side of the risk. Whether or not the corporate is aware, sometimes the risk will be disaggregated into a number of component parts, through the use of FRAs, futures, forwards, options, or their variants, strips, etc. this will create either slices of risk acceptable to counterparties, or to suit the trader's portfolio, or as part of, say a bank's own overall asset/liability management strategy.

Chapter 7

Swaps and Other Derivatives Compared

It is not intended here to go into every 'raspberry ripple', 'bells and whistles' derivative which has been designed, manufactured or synthesised by armies of 'rocket scientists' since the early days of the 'plain vanilla' swap. Two things start as assumptions however: first, through the use of derivatives, it is possible to model, hedge, create, etc most of the balance sheet risks a corporate treasurer is likely to face. Bankers and traders are constantly designing 'rinky dink' variants, to create or meet the demand. Second, every derivative is a variation on, or a combination of, swaps, options or forward contracts (the latter taken to include futures).

The first swap may have been officially done in 1981, but options and forward contracts have been around for much longer. Options were first traded in Amsterdam in the seventeenth century (although they really caught on after the Black-Scholes valuation model was created in 1973).

Forward contracts were in use in the 12th century, if not before and the first formal futures exchange was the Bradford Wool Exchange, which was used for wool futures over 100 years ago. 'Coffee house' business started in London much earlier. Indeed, the first major financial disaster, was 'Tulipomania' in 1637.

The biggest factor recently has been the use of technology. Not only for 'number-crunching' the complex models, but also for coming up with synthesised possibilitiesfor calculating the complex weighted consequences of a new contract or release on the overall balance of the portfolio of a banker or trader, or calculating the duration weighted net exposure of a balance sheet and the effect of a change in interest rates or a shift in the yield curve.

These modelling techniques have also dramatically reduced the opportunities for and size of arbitrages in financial markets for derivatives or their underlying securities.

As mentioned earlier, overall volume in derivatives continues to grow exponentially. Only one decade after swaps had become 'common currency' the global notional amount outstanding of derivatives on the OTC markets alone was estimated at $47.5 trillion (source: BIS Annual Report 1996, as at March 1995).

When one considers that at the same date, ISDA members alone recorded $18 trillion of OTC outstandings and nearly $10 trillion of exchange-traded instruments, it can be seen how difficult and spurious it is to estimate current total volumes. By early 2000, the total outstanding notional amounts of all derivatives (exchange-traded or OTC) may well exceed $200 trillion. Of this total, swaps may represent 75% or more, futures, 15% and options 10%.

For the purpose of this section, we shall simply define and compare with swaps, the four simple models: forwards; FRAs; futures; and options.

Forwards and swaps compared

Forwards are much less common since the arrival of FRAs. A forward deposit is basically a deposit transaction whose terms are agreed now, for value on some agreed future date. The price basis for forwards is the basis of the formula for pricing FRAs and futures. A forward is not like a swap, but can be combined to produce a forward swap (i.e. where the terms of a future swap agreement, for value on a future date, are agreed in advance.)

The forward/forward rate can be derived from the yield curve. For example, we may wish to determine the three-month rate, three-months forward. For this purpose we can compare the notional total cashflows from a six-month deposit effected at the current rate and the cashflow stream from a notional three-month deposit of the same principal, invested at the three-month rate implied by the yield curve three-months hence. By taking the difference between the two, we can calculate the notional three-month rate, three-months forward.

FRAs and swaps compared

An FRA is an agreement to fix a future rate for a single period in the future (e.g. during the term of a loan). An interest rate swap is an agreement whereby two parties exchange all the cashflow streams during the term of the loan. The rate at which the FRA is fixed, will be derived from the forward/forward rate explained earlier, the difference being that a FRA can be bought and sold.

Settlement of the FRA doesn't take place until the start of the interest period and will be a payment between buyer and seller, determined by whether the actual LIBOR fix on the day is higher or lower than the FRA agreed rate. Settlement is the difference discounted to the settlement date from the end of the FRA. For the floating rate payer, therefore, the FRA can therefore be set to be equivalent to the LIBOR fix of one leg of a swap executed for the same future period.

Similarly, for the floating rate receiver (fixed rate payer) who chooses to do so for any particular reason, the LIBOR fix for one leg can be hedged out for an exactly matching period, using a FRA. Whether this results in a net cost or saving will be dependent on timing and the level and shape of the yield curve at the time of the initial swap and the later FRA. If they transacted concurrently, the price of each should be correlated to that portion of the yield curve.

Other comparisons include:
- Both FRAs and IRSs cost nothing up front (although there may be a loss or gain later, depending on movements in and expectations of interest rates);
- Both can be covered by ISDA agreements;
- Settlement for both is by cash receipt or payment (on the interest rate start date for the FRA and the interest payment date for the IRS);
- Both imply and involve counterparty credit exposure;
- FRAs are for a single period (although they can be set up sequentially), whereas IRSs usually cover a number of fixing periods within the term of the loan.

Futures and swaps compared

The history of futures really starts with commodity futures in the 19th century. With currencies being allowed to float freely from 1972, when the Bretton Woods Agreement ceased to be viable, financial futures were born, with the Chicago futures market evolving alongside the previous commodity structures. Exchange rate futures started trading with the establishment of the International Monetary Market in May 1972 and interest rate futures were first traded in October 1975. Share indices followed in 1981 and London (LIFFE) and Far East exchanges were established in the 1980s and 1990s. There are now over 40 such exchanges worldwide.

A financial future is a binding agreement to buy or sell standard quantities of specified financial instruments at prices agreed at the time of the deal, for delivery at specified times in the future. Whilst based on actual or notional instruments, they are not used for the purpose of contracting the instruments themselves. Rather, they are used to create or hedge the equivalent risk, without the need to acquire the underlying principal or commitment.

On the world's leading futures exchanges, a number of contracts are traded in, e.g. short-term interest rates, bonds (e.g. US Treasury Bond, UK, Government Securities, or Gilts), EURO Bonds, Stock Market indices (e.g. FTSE 100), as well as all the major currencies, of course and five year swaps. LIFFE also trades options on futures, e.g. short-term sterling and other European currency deposits. They are traded to pre-fixed settlement dates. Nowadays, most of the contracts are notional, to avoid wild fluctuations in the underlying securities, but also, because there are not normally issued securities with maturity dates that match the traded futures, so notional ones are assumed.

A currency future provides the ability to buy or sell a set amount of a currency against dollars at one of four fixed dates during a year. Unlike other hedging instruments, there is a need to put up a 'margin' (a proportion of the potential losses) and as a contract moves 'out of the money' there may be a need to add further margin.

Among the advantages of futures over swaps, for corporate treasurers: futures do not use up credit lines with counterparties (the credit risk is with the exchange); futures will inevitably be more liquid, because of their traded nature. However, currency volatility has become far greater in the last 20 years and the 'beta' of the exchange future must by definition be even greater than that of the underlying currency. This does not need to be a problem if you have some flexibility over the date you can close out the contract, but the term of contracts is relatively short and, the longer the term, the less the liquidity (although this latter will not be material for most corporates). Nowadays, futures markets tend to drive underlying markets, rather than the opposite.

While swaps are far less liquid than futures, they do offer the flexibility of exactly matching fixing and value date requirements, provided that a counterparty can be found. Also, the liquidity of currency exchanges against the major currencies means that it is possible to raise funds in a major currency and swap to a minor currency, given sufficient flexibility. As the Euro develops, we may see even more opportunities. Raising money in other centres may confer tax or accounting benefits (or cause, or enhance complexity).

In summary, exchange, bond or interest rate futures can always only represent a notional model of the underlying risk, otherwise there might have to be futures contracts for each settlement date, thereby dramatically reducing liquidity and making markets more volatile. Swaps can be precisely matched to the interest rate or currency requirements or commitments, provided one can find a counterparty to take the other side of the risk. Once, this might have been hard, but with the growth of traded portfolios in that banking community, as part of the holistic managed risk, using all appropriate hedging instruments, as well as the assets and liabilities from their own balance sheets, it may often be possible to manufacture a specific risk or hedge as required.

Futures are likely to be used by the bank or corporate as part of a portfolio of risk management instruments, giving added liquidity and flexibility in being able to respond rapidly to increased volatility. Whereas a future can be sold, closing a swap risk requires finding a new counterparty to take the opposite risk, or getting the original party to agree to close or cancel the contract, at a price, one way or the other.

Futures may have equivalent translation risk, transaction risk may be lower, but immediate economic risk may be higher than for swaps, depending on the flexibility for moving in and out of the hedge. The corollary of the greater volatility of futures is the freedom to move in and out of them, as appropriate, based on the depth of the market's liquidity.

With an interest rate swap, the corporate treasurer will typically agree to pay a spread over the given Treasury bond in return for receiving periodic LIBOR payments. The volatility in swap spreads mirrors the volatility in futures. Volatility of swap spreads has increased in recent years. If the treasurer fears that swap spreads may widen, an interest rate swap may be preferable to 'shorting' (selling) the short-term interest rate future.

If spreads are expected to narrow, the future may be the preferred holding position until the desired spread is reached, before locking in the swap. Liquidity of bond markets will also be a consideration, especially with the liquidity of futures. It can be seen, therefore, that apart from changing the nature of financial risk for short-term tactical or speculative reasons, futures will often be used as an adjunct to, or to augment, swaps.

Options and swaps compared

Swaps may usually be used where the corporate treasurer: has a strong view of the future trend in interest rates and has a borrowing requirement or an asset exposure; where the calculated or judged effect of a future adverse rate movement is greater than the consequences of a favourable rate movement; where certainty of future cashflows is a paramount requirement.

Options markets trade volatility of rates or currencies, where the underlying markets trade the rates themselves. Options markets are far more liquid. In currency markets, foreign exchange option contracts have existed since the 1970s, although the nature of options existed from 1860 in Chicago and similar structures were used in ancient China.

An option is the right (but not the obligation), to buy or sell an agreed amount of a specified currency, financial instrument, futures contract, stock index, stock or even swap (swaption), at an agreed price, on or before a pre-determined expiry date. One of the advantages is that, having paid the price of the option, if it does not work out as expected, you can simply walk away from it, whereas if a swap or underlying borrowing or asset deteriorates in value, you are still obligated for the inherent losses during or at the end of the period until the final value date.

Options are both traded on recognised exchanges and OTC (over the counter). As with the future, they do not involve any underlying principal (therefore limiting the exposure) and offer the freedom of choice to exercise the decision or not, but they also offer an incremental cost over and above the cost of the underlying risk (if entered into), as the price of such flexibility. It is not practicable for a treasurer to leave the decision on medium or long-term borrowing until the day when the funds are needed, and also this increases the risk. Futures and options allow the possibility of taking a view on the future course of interest rate or currency movements before the borrowing is effected, including taking an option on the future swap itself (through a swaption or a future on the 5 year swap).

A swap involves entering a contract or contracts involving principal amounts for quite long-terms, which may be difficult to unwind or disengage before maturity, without significant cost (due to illiquidity). Options and futures allow the possibility of either deferring or protecting future decisions at a cost. In the case of futures, the cost may be zero (after settlement of margin) if the movement in rates or currency is favourable during the period until the contract is closed or sold. In the case of options, there is a finite, known, once off cost.

In both cases, this is the premium paid (usually immediately) for ultimate flexibility. In reality, options or variants, and futures, will be used by many treasurers as part of their ongoing asset/liability management process (Remember, any acceptance of risk on one side of the balance sheet may involve creating a naked exposure on the other side).

Among the most attractive options for treasurers as an adjunct, rather than an alternative to swaps, are caps, collars and floors. A **cap** is an interest rate option that provides the purchaser with a guarantee that a floating rate will not rise above a given fixed level. A **floor** guarantees that a rate will not fall below a given level (useful for securing the return on an asset). And a **collar** ensures that a rate will not fall outside a given band of interest rates during the period of the contract. In the latter case, the mechanism is to buy a cap and sell a floor. A collar can be structured so that its cost is zero (depending on the band of rates agreed). Where a cap has been executed at the same rate as the floor rate in a collar, the effect is to fix the rate paid on the floating rate liability at this rate, thereby achieving the same effect as an interest rate swap.

Conclusion

The foregoing does not attempt to be a treatise on the most appropriate instruments to use in various situations. Swaps have become highly flexible and liquid since their first appearance in the 1980s. Since then, markets in OTC and quoted derivatives have developed at an equally explosive rate. Corporate treasurers like the ability to create or manage certainty.

With increased sophistication and the variety of instruments, they can use futures and options to enhance the flexibility of liability or asset portfolios as an adjunct to the widespread use of swaps. They can also be used as a means to defer or speculate on, the future levels of swap rates, or even interest and currency rates themselves.

Forward looking treasurers now use sophisticated asset/liability management techniques for holistic balance sheet management, rather than risk by risk. The infinite flexibility of such risks frequently demands the use of a portfolio of derivative techniques rather than one by one, risk by risk, usually because managing a discreet risk can create a corresponding unmatched exposure elsewhere.

Chapter 8

Examples
The use of interest rate and currency swaps

The following are simplified illustrations of typical swap transactions:

Figure 1 - Simple Interest Rate Swap

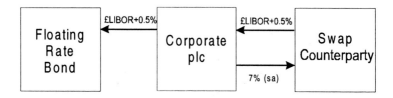

In the above example, a corporate has issued a floating rate bond, on which six-month LIBOR plus 0.5% is payable. It finds a counterparty (probably a bank), which is prepared to receive 7% fixed rate payments, semi-annually, in exchange for paying six-month LIBOR.

In simple terms, the corporate has achieved a fixed rate semi-annual cost of funds of 7%, which presumably it would not have been able to achieve on its own name with fixed rate borrowing.

Figure 2 - Coupon Swap (Cross currency interest rate swap)

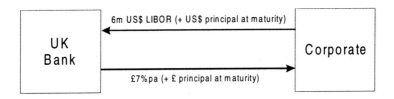

This shows one possible combination of the interest rate and currency swap.

Figure 3 - Elements of a Currency Swap

Initial exchange of commitments

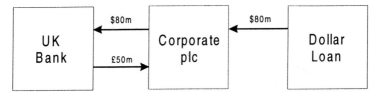

Basis of periodic payments

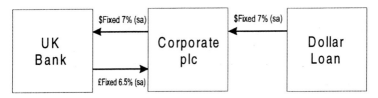

Maturity and reversal of commitments

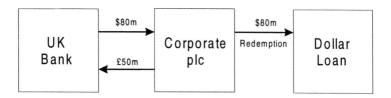

This example shows the capital exchanges, as well as the swapped interest payments.

Figure 4 - Arbitraging counterparty credit ratings

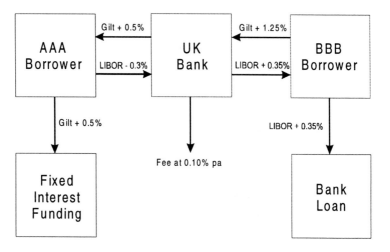

In Figure 4 above, it is assumed that the AAA rated corporate, at Gilt plus 0.5%, would pay 1% less than a BBB corporate, at Gilt plus 1.5%, to raise funds in the fixed rate market; but the BBB corporate, at 0.35%, would only have to pay 0.25% more than the AAA corporate for six-month floating rate funds. The swap transactions above, achieve cheaper funds for both in their approved medium of payment, leaving a 10 basis point fee for the bank which intermediates. AAAborrower pays LIBOR-0.3% floating and BBB borrower pays 1.25% for fixed rate, so both gain.

Figure 5 - Match Funding Fixed Rate Mortgages (1991)

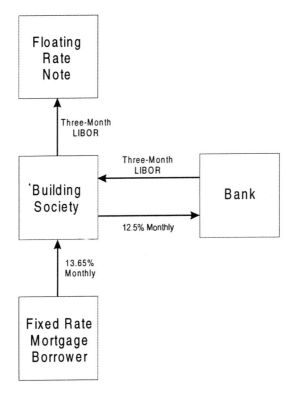

(Guaranteed margin = 1.15% over LIBOR)

Figure 5 shows exactly how N&P was able to fund its first fixed rate mortgage product in 1991. The margin was less than for conventional business, but the marketing and administrative expense was also lower. Now, fixed rate, capped and other variations are commonplace in the mortgage market.

Figure 6 - Zero Coupon Swap

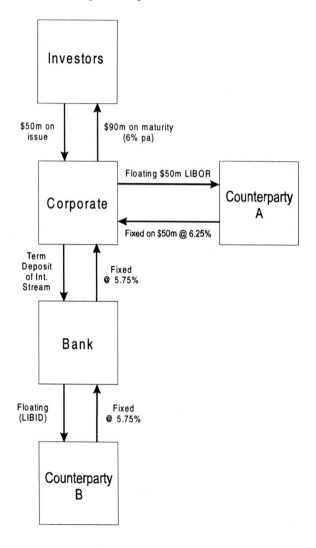

In Figure 6, a corporate issues a 10 year zero-coupon stock with a maturity value of $90m, receiving $50m on issue. It enters into a $50m swap with counterparty A, receiving fixed rate at 6.25% in exchange for floating LIBOR. It has achieved floating rate funding. Meanwhile, in order to plan for the $90m maturity payment, it invests the stream of fixed rate payments with a bank on term deposit (the bank having swapped to pay LIBID against the matching fixed rate receipt).

Figure 7 - Basis Swap

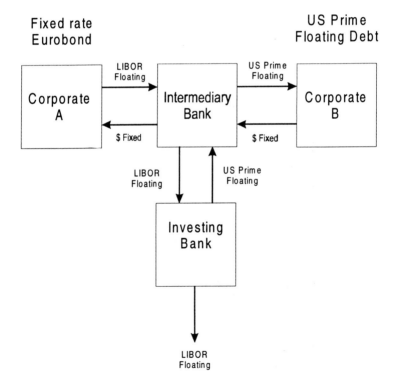

In Figure 7, an investing bank has a Prime yielding asset which it wishes to hedge into floating LIBOR. Corporate A has issued a $ fixed rate bond which it wishes to swap to LIBOR floating.

Corporate B has US Prime floating debt on which it wishes to fix the cost. An intermediary bank effects these two swap, netting the exposure by effecting a third LIBOR/Prime swap with the investing bank.

Figure 8 - Equity Swap

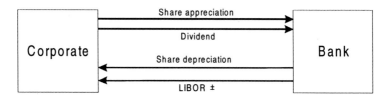

In Figure 8, a corporate swaps the uncertain return on an equity investment for floating rate LIBOR. Note that an integral part of the swap is that the hedging bank compensates for any loss in the equity value.

*Figure 9 - Combined Cross Currency Swap and
        Differential Swap*

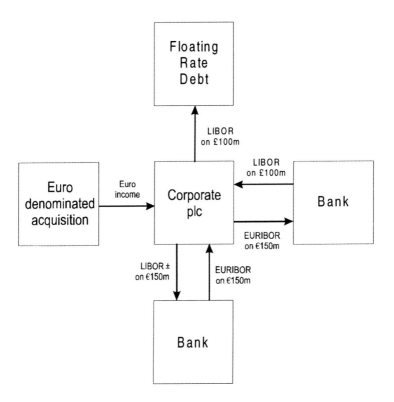

In Figure 9, the corporate has achieved a net cost of LIBOR±
payable in Euros, to fund its Euro denominated acquisition.

Chapter 9

Exposure, Valuation, Management and Capital Adequacy

With any swap, there are two main types of risk: market risk; and credit risk. The market risk is based on the possibility that exposure to a particular interest rate or currency risk can result in an actual or expected loss. Credit risk is related to the fact that, where a particular interest rate or currency exposure produces an anticipated gain, a counterparty defaults, leaving an actual loss.

Estimating exposure

Swaps are not quoted market instruments. They are dealt with over the counter (OTC). When they were first created, they were held to maturity and the fixed or floating-rate payers, for example, simply received and paid their respective cash flow streams. The cash or present value of these streams would produce a 'gain' or 'loss' for the respective payer, against what they received, crystallising their judgement of interest rates over the swap period. Nowadays, it is wise, if not mandatory, to value these anticipated gains or losses over time, especially using, e.g. 'mark-to-market' techniques.

The difficulty inherent in using mark to market in terms of swaps, is how to evaluate the market risk at the outset of the swap. On the day it is executed, the net present value of the risk must by definition be zero (for a swap at current market rates). Every day after this, it will vary. This takes no account of the shape of and possible changes to the yield curve. From this understanding, it is possible to calculate the present value of a basis point (PVBP).

It would be an unusual set of circumstances if PVBP was zero also. Therefore, even at the outset, there is a calculable risk represented by the present value of a one basis point change in the market. Simple mark-to-market will not pick this up. Furthermore, it will only produce an exposure when rates imply a positive value on the swap. We need to take mark-to-market further, therefore, to take account of interest rates implied from the yield curve, i.e., forward rates, not just current rates.

Another difficulty is that, if the yield curve was downward sloping, this would imply future gain for the floating rate payer, but this once again overlooks the risk implied by PVBP and/or possible changes in the shape of the yield curve. We need to find a way to take account of uncertainty, therefore. This can be done by calculating the distribution of all possible swap rates at a given point in time, using option pricing methods. From such a distribution, it is possible to calculate the total probability of exposure.

When applied to the weighted average of all swap rates above the original swap rate, it is possible to calculate the size, or value of the exposure. Once again, while simple NPV methods may appear to imply no market risk, both PVBP and the probability basis are likely to produce a different picture. Why would we wish to do this? For reasons of prudence and accounting purposes (see later).

When we come to consider a cross-currency swap as well, we have to take account of the risks inherent in the interest rates of both currencies *and* the risks in the currency rate, including the likelihood that a change in any one of these will have a direct effect in the value of the others.

While the present text does not allow for the detailed maths of these considerations (there are both specialised texts and computer generated models to perform this task), it is clear that the combined market risk of a cross-currency swap is not just likely to be greater than the three constituent risks, but also, even when the NPV calculations appear to give zero risk, this would be oversimplifying and overlooking the true risk.

The latter includes the probability of interest rate and currency changes, as well as changes to the shapes of the respective yield curves, the interrelationship of the two currencies over time and the correlated interrelationship between the two sets of domestic interest rates, as affected through the currency changes.

Credit exposure

An important consideration arising from the above methods for evaluating market exposure, is the implications for credit exposure. The latter arises out of actual or anticipated gains. Each corporate treasurer should have a policy of credit limits for counterparties, ideally taking account of the capital reserves of the corporate and those of the counterparty.

Setting these for deposits or 'globally' may be a fairly straight-forward exercise. Complications arise when we take account of the actual or expected values of credit exposure arising out of outstanding swaps, especially as these can vary minute by minute, let alone day to day.

Credit lines are set according to overall maximum potential exposure, credit by credit. The expected exposure resulting from a given swap can be calculated at the outset, using the approaches outlined above and these will be factored into the totals for each counterparty (for all types of market and commercial risk).

So, for example, if Barclays is the counterparty for all the outstanding swaps, the calculated credit risk from these will be added to that of, say investments and deposits in Barclays originated assets, to determine whether the global ceiling for Barclays has been, or is likely to be exceeded. This calculation will need to be done day to day, as the risk varies. To be highly sophisticated, one could also factor in exposures calculated from default probability tables, which take account of the variation of risk in relation to different credit ratings.

Risks of these sort do not often occur in the case of swaps, however and , while one should not take the ostrich's perspective, at the very least one would wish to take account of full value risk and market risk. Full value risk, or settlement risk, is that which arises from the non-simultaneous exchange of assets (e.g. spot forex transactions, deposits, uncollateralised investments and securities trades where settlement is not on a delivery versus payment basis).

Market risk, which we are concerned with here, is the loss which may arise, due to a gain resulting from a change in price in the underlying asset or liability, if the counterparty fails to deliver part or whole value of the gain. This would certainly be relevant to interest rate or currency swaps and swaptions (in the latter case, the buyer only).

Current value

In July 1996, a discussion paper was produced by the UK Accounting Standards Board, suggesting the use of current market value in accounting for financial instruments in the balance sheet. This was strongly resisted by the Association of Corporate Treasurers, with the result that when FRS13 appeared, while it had been agreed that there was a need for improved disclosure of the risk profile and explanation of policies and strategies for holding or issuing financial instruments", in general terms the approach on exposure was to value on a "highly aggregated" basis. The accounting treatment is discussed at greater length in the following chapter.

There will remain a dichotomy between those who believe it is possible to value the net worth of the balance sheet in current market value terms, taking account of interest rate changes implied by the forward yield curve and those who believe that the latter is spurious in terms of not representing the actual eventuality of interest rates and that a balance sheet based on current market value is just a snapshot at a point in time. With time, interest rates and currency rates constantly changing this is neither real nor representative of the likely outcome.

We shall argue later, however, that at least an internal duration weighted view of the effect of changing rates on net worth and an awareness and understanding of VAR, is fundamental for the proactive treasurer/finance director and a source of reassurance for the informed non-executive director. To have these evaluations emerge into the marketplace is to invite even more volatility in share prices.

Management of exposure

It would be unusual in this day and age to manage a particular exposure in isolation. The computer tools exist to value any discrete or total net risk position, whether involving swaps, options, futures, FRAs or derivatives of the same.

With this sophistication, together with the general approach to balance sheet management outlined in Chapter 12, it is possible for the corporate treasurer or banker to evaluate the net present value worth of the whole balance sheet, to calculate the VAR (value at risk) and to determine the effect on present value net worth of a change of one basis point in interest rates, or one 'pip' in a currency, at any time. A daily review of this, together with an awareness of the major components of the balance sheet and the key factors which would produce the greatest incremental change is sufficient for the treasurer to pursue a total risk management approach.

Capital adequacy

For corporates, capital adequacy is usually a consequence of successful trading. While a fresh issue of equity provides new capital resources, the only valid reason is if the capital is needed for investment or acquisition purposes. Fresh capital can in the interim be invested in the money markets until it is used, but shareholders expect a growing return, made up of the combination of an increasing dividend and appreciation in the capital value of shares. Neither is likely to happen in the longer term if equity just sits in the bank.

GEC pursued a policy of investing its spare capital in Gilts for many years and, while it was safe, the unexciting return it produced led to the shares of the company underperforming the FTSE 100. Capital can of course be damaged or wiped out by bad business or speculation, of course and a degree of adequacy will always be prudent. However, the main source for corporates should be retained after tax profits and where there is more than enough, we are seeing a growing number simply repaying unneeded capital to enhance net shareholder value.

For banks and financial institutions (such as building societies), however, it is a different matter. They exist primarily as lending and investing institutions. Whether as retail or commercially based operations, they rely on either or both customer and investor confidence to remain in business. They take and engage in more risky business than many corporates (especially where they are running trading and/or derivatives books) and need to pay more heed to capital needs.

Both corporates and banks can be rated by the rating agencies and, while this gives a reliable (albeit largely historical) indicator of creditworthiness, in terms of creditor, capital and interest payments, it is not sufficient for financial institutions which represent the backbone of the financial economy and the medium through which money and derivatives markets are sustained.

Accordingly, they are regulated by central banks and one of the fundamental planks of that regulation is capital adequacy. The latter was a straightforward matter before derivatives. Many banks made a steady living (except during the secondary banking crisis of the. 1970s) and the nature of their core business was less risky than it is now. Although most engaged in foreign exchange transactions and had outstanding positions, to intermediate 'in markets for the benefit of their customers and the system as a whole, they were not then engaged in derivatives, whether for hedging or trading purposes.

Various types of derivatives have various potential scales of exposure. Banks now have no excuse not to be aware of both discrete and holistic net exposure and capital adequacy requirements have increased accordingly. Central banks as a group have become more concerned about both the scale and growth in volatility and the proportion of business now conducted 'off-balance sheet'.

This was brought home clearly with the crash of 1987, with so many trades being computer driven. They have become a little more sanguine since, hoping that Barings type lessons have been learned, recognising the importance for world trade and becoming more sophisticated themselves in the understanding and regulation of derivatives operations. With such a huge volume of world trade now driven and/or supported by swaps-related transactions, there is a delicate balance to be achieved between regulation and facilitation.

The banks are the most sophisticated in their use and understanding of derivatives and have the tools to value individual and total positions, whether on- and off-balance sheet. Capital adequacy requirements world-wide have now been extended by the need for consideration of these positions as well as the weightings applied to the traditional lending and investing business. Whether this would be sufficient in the event of a major loss of confidence in financial markets world-wide, with the inter-relationship of banks' positions, especially through derivatives driven transactions, is one test of the world banking system we would not like to experience.

Chapter 10

Accounting and Tax

It is not within the scope of the present text, to discuss the overall accounting for derivatives (except en passant), or the varying treatments and requirements in other financial centres. Each has their own regulations and accounting requirements. It would be reasonable however to use the UK recommendations as a benchmark, however, as they strike a balance between accounting purity and objectivity.

Failures such as Barings were not down to accounting treatment, so much as management, accountability, supervision, internal reporting, separation of function and control. It is in the nature of accounting, rather than reporting, that the information is usually some way out of date by the time it is read by interested parties. In the meantime, they are entitled to rely on directors' determination and supervision of internal policies, management practices and procedures, to avoid the possibility of disaster or material risk to, or actual diminution of, net worth.

The main accounting steers in recent years have come from the British Bankers Association (BBA) and the Accounting Standards Board (ASB). We shall deal only with those aspects which directly or indirectly affect accounting for swaps.

BBA SORP 1996

The Statement of Recommended Accounting Practice on Derivatives was produced in February 1996. Its application is for the accounting treatment and disclosure of derivatives in the accounts of UK and Irish banks. Its scope included "all interest rate, exchange rate, equity and commodity related derivatives, including...swaps..." It defined swaps as "customised OTC instruments under which two parties exchange payments at specified intervals over a specified period of time. They are usually based on interest or exchange rates, but can also be linked to equity or commodity prices."

The valuation and income recognition rules included aimed "to ensure that derivatives held by banks are reflected in the primary financial statements according to the purpose for which they are held." The accruals and prudence concepts of general accounting were also to be applied, especially in terms of not taking account of unrealised profit or revenue. However, "where all of the costs and risks associated with a particular earnings flow arise in the period being reported, then all of the revenue generated by a transaction should be recognised."

It saw, inter alia, swaps being entered into for one of three reasons: "customer facilitation; proprietary; and hedging" a bank's own risks. "(Swaps) held for customer facilitation or proprietary reasons should be measured at fair value and those held for hedging purposes should be valued on the same basis as the underlying asset, liability, position or cash flow.... It should be presumed that (swaps) are trading transactions unless it can be demonstrated that they constitute non-trading transactions." (More often with swaps than other derivatives). "Derivatives qualifying as non-trading are those entered into for the purpose of matching or eliminating risk from potential movements in interest rates, exchange rates and/or market price inherent in the assets, liabilities, positions or cash flows being hedged....This approach is necessary to enable financial statements to reflect the way in which banks manage their risk."

Swaps, being non-trading transactions, "should be measured on an accruals basis equivalent to that used for the underlying asset, liability, position or cash flow." The general principle adopted was to look for 'fair value' in valuing derivatives.

When it came to credit risk, the SORP required that "banks should provide an analysis of counterparty credit risk for all...OTC...contracts", based on "net replacement cost analysed between financial institutions...and non-financial institutions." This should be augmented by "a credit risk maturity analysis of exposures arising from OTC...contracts." As with FRED13, it was eventually concluded that "there is still a good deal of ground to be covered before a common basis for disclosing market risk could be established", while requiring "quantitative information about market risk." Finally, in relation to swaps, "gains and losses on non-trading hedges of anticipated transactions that have been deferred in the balance sheet should be disclosed..."

Finally, "banks should provide a statement including: an explanation of their use of derivative instruments;...a discussion of the bank's risk management policies...; and a discussion on how derivatives are used in asset and liability management."

Accounting for swaps

In principle, there is nothing to stop the finance director of either a corporate, bank or financial institution going further than current accounting guidance, providing they are not in fundamental breach of such guidance and are not disclosing or operating in a way which might be prejudicial to their commercial operations, especially on a 'going concern' and 'true and fair view' basis. Any organisation which wins the wide approval of the public in general and markets in particular in relation to its management and implementation of sound, risk-based operation, is more likely to enhance its perceived value than detract from it, provided that it does not make a rod for its own back.

Fortunately, with swaps being non-traded instruments, (not including swap futures), there is less potential for damage or wildly fluctuating net worth. Nevertheless, some evidence for prudent, objective policies and sound management decisions to protect ongoing enterprise and net worth is highly desirable. The general principle adopted in the accounting recommendations is to take a high level view of policies, procedures and value at risk (VAR).

The growth in the volume and value of outstandings of derivatives in general and swaps in particular, together with their fluctuating notional values, related to volatility in financial markets led, not surprisingly, to the Accounting authorities taking an interest. In 1989, the IASC (International Accounting Standards Committee) took the lead. This was welcome particularly because of its international acceptability as an authority to recommend appropriate accounting treatment.

The questions were, however, which instruments should be brought into consideration and which organisations should be targeted. In the former case, the most pressing examples were traded instruments and obviously banks would have the greatest need for proper accounting by virtue of both their visibility and exposure. The other practical consideration was whether the guidance would cover all financial instruments or subsets, such as swaps, options or futures.

The IASC was established in 1973 and since that time, it has made several recommendations, while each individual country has its own accounting and regulatory framework. The UK has the ASB, while in the US, the FASB (Financial Accounting Standards Board) recommends best practice in accounting and the SEC (Securities and Exchange Commission) lays down regulation.

IAS 30 (Disclosures in the Financial Statements of Banks and Similar Financial Institutions, August 1990), set the tone in terms of defining which monetary assets and liabilities must be included in financial statements, but it is the local Accounting Standards which have taken accounting forward in member countries, as far as possible towards the 'true and fair view' in accounting for derivatives, such as swaps.

By 1996, the debate on accounting in the UK was raging, the crux of which was the dichotomy between accounted value and economic value, together with the ongoing and perpetually revaluing nature of derivative transactions. This is even more so for non-traded instruments, such as swaps, where values have to be derived from a forward yield curve, whereas traded instruments have a market price.

On a given balance sheet date, swaps can be notionally valued, but their only true value is the settlement value to close the swap on that day, if a quote could be obtained. Clearly, the loss or gain associated with the early termination of a swap should be crystallised in the profit and loss account, but very few people were going to agree on even current value as a basis for accounting for outstanding swaps in a side note, let alone the balance sheet per se.

The outcome was FRS 13, published in September 1998, which watered down the original proposals of the ASB. It applied to "any entity which has any of its capital instruments listed or publicly traded on a stock exchange or market or is a bank or similar institution or a banking or similar group."

As far as swaps are concerned, the relevant disclosures are:

"cumulative aggregate unrecognised gains and losses in respect of hedges of future transactions, and encouraged disclosure on sensitivities to market price risk (e.g. to interest rates, currency movements);

fair value of financial assets and liabilities, without requiring fair value: to be used in balance sheets; or to be disclosed if this is not practicable;

there is no longer a requirement for separate disclosure of fair value of financial assets and financial liabilities which are not traded on organised markets (taken to include swaps);"

together with other more general statements.

Finally, it should be noted that some differences exist between FRS 13 and IAS 32, including in the latter case the requirement to disclose amounts, timing, certainty of future cashflows of each class of financial instrument and numerical disclosures on exposures to credit risk; together with disclosure and an explanation wherever an entity is carrying 'one or more financial assets at an amount in excess of fair value."

In summary, therefore, the accounting requirements for banks, in relation to swaps and non-traded instruments are hardly onerous, beyond the requirement to capture historical consequences and cumulative unrecognised losses or gains. For corporates they are almost non-existent. Nevertheless, statements on risk policies, practices and procedures are becoming more widespread in annual reports and the fundamentals of accounting - true and fair view, going concern, accruals, consistency and prudence, remain for consideration. The debate will continue indefinitely, with the pace being set by best practice and the most skilled risk managers.

Taxation considerations

General taxation considerations are taken into account in as far as they impact the overall taxation of recognised gains and losses arising from swap transactions. By 1985, the growth in swaps business was being mirrored by the growth in self-appointed swaps tax experts. The main reason was the change from a transaction to hedge a risk, to a product in its own right. Once swaps became widely 'traded' they were going to attract the attention of the tax authorities. At the time, though, withholding tax was troubling finance directors as much as the domestic tax treatment of elements of a swap transaction, such as fees, in the case of currency swaps.

In the UK, the Finance Act 1994, made the tax treatment of swaps much more certain. Before that time, periodic payments under an interest rate swap were only deductible by concession, not under specific legislation, other swap payments creating only capital losses or were effectively not deductible at all.

The new Act, closely linked to the tax regime for foreign exchange gains and losses meant that from March 1995:

in relation to qualifying interest rate and currency contracts, companies would be taxed on cash inflows arising under such contracts and would receive tax relief on cash outflows following the accounting treatment (either mark-to-market or accruals accounting was permitted);

the revenue/capital distinction which had caused problems in the past would disappear, with both trading and non-trading gains and losses recognised as revenue items;

net gains would be taxable, with net losses being offsettable against other taxable profits in the company on a current year basis Unused losses could be carried back for a maximum of three years, or carried forward against future non-trading foreign exchange or financial instrument gains.

The new rules did much to clear the air and increased the certainty of the tax treatment of swaps and other hedging instruments, while also opening up economic anomalies, including arbitrage opportunities, especially during the transition period! The anomalies between international accounting treatments and tax regimes, while converging to some degree, remain as a threat or opportunity to the informed treasurer or arbitrageur.

Chapter 11

Case Studies and Disasters

No doubt little known problems and complications litter the history of the inexorable development of swaps markets. At the outset, it was hard enough to find counterparties to create them, let alone have them fail. Now, the whole derivatives industry is highly sophisticated, with higher incremental or absolute risk in some of the other, especially traded, instruments (as Nick Leeson demonstrated infamously).

Swaps, even of foreign exchange commitments, are relatively straightforward transactions, whose main purpose remains to improve the efficiency of borrowings in international loan and bond markets. Currency swaps have, in no small measure, contributed to facilitating the growth of global trade.

The main area of risk in swaps, therefore, would appear to be credit risk and/or the failure of a counterparty. Even here, with so many banks trading or intermediating swaps and international credit ratings prevalent, the credit risk should be limited. In this section, we shall review the two most spectacular swaps based failures, together with practical illustrations of how swaps have worked well for corporates.

Catastrophe - Hammersmith & Fulham

The most famous UK based swaps failure related to Local Authorities (LAs), and specifically the London Borough of

Hammersmith and Fulham, which repudiated its swaps transactions once it found out that they were technically *ultra vires* (beyond their powers or authority). The result sent a shock wave through UK markets and damaged the impression of sterling credits overseas.

Huge numbers of banks lost money, as other LAs became implicated and the transactions of other counterparties came into question, such as Building Societies and other UK public bodies. It was some time before the interest rate swaps market re-established its equilibrium and questionable credits were able to re-enter the market, having assured their capacity to contract swaps.

Yet, only months before, the growth of the UK interest rates swaps market was being driven along on the crest of a confident wave of LAs, changing the basis of their interest rate liabilities, on the strength of a bullish view of interest rates, ostensibly to save their ratepayers money.

In June 1989, a Director of a major firm of brokers and ex-treasurer of a major London Borough, wrote in *The Treasurer* (official organ of the Association of Corporate Treasurers), *"there is no Act of Parliament which either specifically permits or prevents local authorities entering into interest rate management agreements"* and *"the Audit Commission, which having taken counsel's opinion, took the view that swaps were lawful provided the transactions related to specific debt obligations on the authorities' books."*

With £56,000 million of outstanding debt, most of it fixed rate and an increasing proportion over seven years, some LA treasurers were following their private sector counterparts in hedging their exposures, using swaps at first, followed by swaptions, caps, floors and collars, futures and FRAs. Some had been hedging the risk of interest rate rises by swapping into fixed rate. But many had taken advantage of growing private sector demand for fixed rate funding, by swapping for the floating rate on outstanding medium term liabilities. At the time of the article, the legality of hedging at all was being tested in the courts.

Much of the market became suspended, when the District Auditor of Hammersmith and Fulham challenged the legality of these transactions. By that time, the Borough was heavily exposed, having filled up lines of credit with one bank after another. The significance was not for them alone, however, as many other LAs had jumped on the bandwagon, by the time dealing was stopped. The uncertainty did not stop with open transactions, as the *ultra vires* ruling was likely to be retrospective even for completed deals and, even where LAs had gained from such transactions, their counterparties might be able to reopen them on the same *ultra vires* basis.

Banking auditors and Finance Directors had another headache in terms of deciding on provisions, accruals and contingencies, until matters were decided. In the event, the High Court ruled all the derivative transactions unlawful, which "shocked and angered the City but has also created an area of uncertainty as the wider implications of the judgement unfold." (Rohan Courtney, State bank of New South Wales).

Many LAs had been using swaps to augment revenue in a constrained financial environment, including the receipt of front-end premiums on large swaps, treated on an in-year basis, together with a temporary reduction in interest rate commitments before rising rates set in. The national Audit Commission had appeared to approve of these deals, subject to one or two provisos. This was in addition to the legal opinion of counsel that had ruled that swaps were legal if used as part of debt management.

Unfortunately, counsel had to change their opinion when it was realised that Hammersmith and Fulham had entered into 600 or so swap transactions, mainly swaps and swaptions, with a notional value of £6 billion. By March 1989, this had been halved to c£3 billion, but this dwarfed the authority's actual borrowings of under £400 million - it had been trading in a huge way. To a lesser extent, so had 76 other LAs!

The fallout was substantial and widespread. One fear was that LAs' would not be able to borrow in the marketplace, leading to possible insolvency as the Bank of England and HM Treasury are not 'lenders of last resort'. Quickly, other fears emerged. More than 70 banks stood to lose £500 million or more, a fifth to Hammersmith. All banks had suspended and placed on review, the *vires* of other non-corporate government regulated institutions and public bodies. Both foreign banks and the Bank itself were concerned that the situation might permanently damage London's reputation as a financial centre, especially as it had been believed that the UK government underwrote the LAs.

Eventually, the mess was sorted out, at a considerable cost to the banks. Many institutions found it difficult to borrow other than short-term funds for some time. The PWLB (a lending arm of government) had to help out in the event and some treasurers were 'assigned to other duties'. The fact that it is a distant memory now, unheard of in many parts of the world, is a testimony to the London financial community to regulate itself - except Barings!

Catastrophe - Gibson Greetings vs Bankers Trust

This case is written up in many other places, but the reference here is from Robin Kendall's book, *Risk Management for Executives* (FT Pitman, 1998).

Gibson's business is the manufacture and sale of greetings cards and gift wrappings. Between November 1991 and early 1994, derivatives became the 'tail that wagged the dog', following an innocuous entry into the use of swaps. In May 1991, the company had issued a $50m series of fixed rate notes with maturities from 1995 to 2001. After their issue, Gibson became concerned at declining interest rates and, in the absence of the ability to prepay the notes, decided to enter into interest rate swaps to reduce the interest payable.

Its chosen partner was Bankers Trust Securities Corp. A master swap agreement was reached in November 1991 and Gibson entered into two-year and five-year 'plain vanilla' interest rate swaps, each for $30m. By July 1992, things had gone well and both swaps had been cancelled, with Gibson receiving a payment from BTSC of $260,000.

From then on, BTSC proposed and Gibson accepted, a series of 25 increasingly complicated deals or amendments.

Without the capability to understand, let alone value, many of these deals, Gibson remained in a state of 'blissful' ignorance as to the extent of the growing losses. On 23 February 1994, BTSC informed Gibson that the value of its derivatives portfolio was minus $8m, two days later nearly $14m, by which time it was actually over $16m! Gibson called time and sued BTSC. Eventually the *Commodities Futures Trading Commission* found BTSC guilty of fraudulent misrepresentation and omission and they were fined $10m.

One could question whether Gibson should even have entered into the original swap transactions, or closed them (as each decision represents a position taken on the overall balance sheet). They appear neither to have understood nor supervised the later transactions. Even though these were increasingly complex structures, nevertheless, this case shows the ease with which a corporate could be drawn into totally unfamiliar territory, despite starting with plain vanilla swaps, especially as it achieved a material gain from its first foray.

Let me repeat - with the exception mainly of banks with traded books, or speculators, derivatives are immensely powerful instruments to hedge balance sheet risk, protecting longer term net worth. We shall see in the next chapter the importance of the right corporate perspective on risk and the recommended approach to balance sheet management.

Other Case Studies

There are innumerable daily examples of how corporates can use derivatives to manage risk and to facilitate borrowing, liability or asset management. Some successful ones are included below:

Eurotunnel

Eurotunnel was entirely private sector funded. A £6.8bn floating rate debt was syndicated in 1987 and 1990. The Board became concerned about the possibility of rising interest rates and an increasing proportion of fixed rate debt was sought. By 1991, it was felt that interest rate swaps should be used, but riskiness of the project at first limited these to two-year swaps, mainly because of constraints on its bankers' facilities.

Other possibilities were considered, including interest rate caps. Eventually, by September 1993, after exhaustive risk analysis by the company, its bankers and several economists, Eurotunnel was able to complete the first swap deals, helped by falling interest rates.

By early 1994, £1bn of swaps had been transacted and although the deals moved 'out of the money' as rates fell further, incurring £16m margin calls, swap rates then moved sharply higher as US interest rates rose, the money was recouped and the certainty of debt cost had been achieved.

It should be stressed that margin calls are not a normal feature of swaps, but the use of a feature which was common on futures exchanges, to 'insure' the bankers, was the key factor which unlocked the ability for Eurotunnel to achieve its swaps goals.

The World Bank and IBM

One of the most famous swap deals is the one that is credited as marking the start of the currency swaps market. In August 1981, the World Bank swapped $290 million of fixed rate debt for Swiss franc˙and Deutschemark denominated liabilities of IBM. The World Bank achieved lower cost Swiss franc and Deutschemark debt than it could even borrow in its own name, because it had borrowed so often in these two markets that it was having to pay a premium.

Meanwhile, IBM, with a good name in these markets and wanting cheap dollars, issued bonds in both and matched the World Bank swap requirements.

Chapter 12

Balance Sheet and Asset/Liability Management

We live in a holistic age. The evolution of swaps and other derivatives was largely transaction driven. Corporates had specific currency or interest rate risks whose nature they wished to change, in order to achieve greater certainty or control. Characteristically, finance directors prefer relative certainty of revenues, costs and the value of assets and liabilities, in order to achieve predictable profits and returns.

A certain, modest gain, enhancing shareholder returns, is by and large preferable to the prospect of a much greater gain, bought at the cost of substantially greater risk. In the Hammersmith and Fulham debacle rafts of swaps were entered into, in order to reduce local authority costs, but the inherent risks were greater. As interest rates fall, the chance of a rise increases, exponentially. Shareholders in companies want progressive performance, without setbacks. Unhedged risks and speculation, coupled with accident of timing, can lead to unpredictable performance.

The evolution of the science of derivatives accompanied a total view of risks. In the late 1980s, it was paralleled by the growth of the art of asset/liability management, or (total) balance sheet management.

Asset/liability management

The simple principle of asset/liability management is that a specific liability or group of liabilities notionally funds each asset. The 'banker's sin' is to fund long-term assets from short-term liabilities. In addition, if the FD could convert all assets into fixed return and all liabilities to fixed cost, profit can be assured. The conversions can be achieved using commodity, interest rate, currency, asset and other derivatives. It may be unexciting, but it minimises predictability.

This approach is unnecessarily rigid, but it overlooks one important concept - that of the time value of assets and liabilities. It also ignores the flexibility afforded by using floating rate liabilities matched to floating rate assets. Much of the early swap business was either to convert fixed rate liabilities into floating rate, by nature, or to turn unpredictable foreign currency risks into common domestic currency risks, for both assets and liabilities.

Balance sheet management

Where the early use of swaps was focused on managing or neutralising specific risks, the art of balance sheet management is based on looking at the balance sheet as a whole. Simply matching each asset with an underlying liability of equivalent domestic currency value is not sufficient. It may be unnecessarily cumbersome or complex; it reduces the flexibility of the balance sheet and its consequent value generation; most important, it may overlook the consequence of time.

The organisation may have £10m property assets, funded by $16m of five-year, dollar based floating rate liabilities. The dollars may be swapped into sterling, but there will be interim payment periods within the five-year term. The currency risk may have been removed, leaving an interest rate or basis risk. The floating rate may be swapped to produce a fixed rate cost.

Property assets are normally deemed to be fixed rate in nature (leaving aside depreciation and deterioration considerations, normally picked up through the revenue account). So, the fixed rate nature is matched, but only for five years, when there is a·refunding risk, related to what happens to interest rates and currency rates in the meantime.

Swaps programmes are now extending out to 25 years and more, especially as we appear to have returned to a period of relatively stable and relatively low interest rates and inflation. Even so, swap spreads have risen alarmingly in recent years, due to international political or economic difficulties (e.g. Russian devaluation, Latin American and Asian economic crises, etc.)

Looking shorter, as one asset or liability matures, it needs to be replaced and/or hedged by another, in variable market places. Supply and demand factors can mean that the precise requirements can not easily be matched.

So emerged the concept of duration. Together with the sophisticated, computer based, mathematical models of risk, duration based asset/liability management started to move corporations closer to total balance sheet management.

The principle of duration

To take a gross simplification, supposing a corporation has a balance sheet as follows:

Assets	**£000s**	**Liabilities**	**£000s**
Cash	28	Creditors (ave life 1.1/2mths)	16
Debtors (ave life 3mths)	20	Loans (ave o/s life 2yrs)	4
Stocks (ave life 6mths)	20	Bonds (ave o/s life 8yrs)	80
Plant (ave life 5yrs)	27		
Property (notional life 100yrs)	5		
Total Assets	100	Total Liabilities	100

Calculating the time weighted average of the balance sheet, the 'duration' is:

Assets: Cash (28 x 0 = 0) + Debtors (20 x 0.25 = 5) + Stocks (20 x 0.5 = 10) + Plant (27 x 5 = 135) + Property (5 x 100 = 500)
Total = 650

Liabilities: Creditors (16 x 0.125 = 2) + Loans (4 x 2 = 8) + Bonds (80 x 8 = 640)
Total = 650

This is a simple view of the principle of duration. By time-weighting the assets and liabilities, we can balance the time value of risk. The 'ages' of assets and liabilities above, equate to the cashflow dates for each, i.e. when each will mature or fall due. Of course, property has been given a notional maturity, for the sake of this example. In reality, more science will be used to age the asset.

Frederick Macaulay was the first to develop the duration concept, while seeking a correct measure for the life of a bond.
To put all bonds on an equal footing, he notionally converted
coupon bond life into an equally risky zero coupon bond.
The principle can be applied to any cash inflow or outflow, so
that each can be turned into the 'term to maturity' of a zero
coupon bond.

Treating each assets or liability in the balance sheet as if it
were a coupon bond and computing the term to maturity of an
equivalent zero coupon bond, 'standardises' the whole balance
sheet. Each result represents the price weighted maturity.

These can be summed, to give the total weighted duration of
assets and of liabilities. The net, either way is the overall duration mismatch. Through sophisticated computer simulation,
the hedges or transactions required to balance the duration
match can be computed.

Swaps are of real value in effecting this in practice, but also,
as with other derivatives, the use of swaps, especially where
they are being used to rebase liabilities in and out of fixed rate
exposure, taking a view on interest rates, can mean that the ap-
parent hedging out of a particular interest rate risk, may put
the whole duration match of the balance sheet out of kilter.
Furthermore, as interest rates vary and maturities shrink, from
day to day, these factors can also change the net value of the
balance sheet.

By the early 1990s, asset/liability management was quite
sophisticated. Even building societies were using duration

matching to manage the daily net balance sheet exposure, resulting in higher credit ratings and eased capital requirements.

While the latter is not regulated for corporates, varying balance sheet exposures have a direct bearing on the earning capacity of the balance sheet, VAR and ultimately shareholder value. Whether or not one has to mark-to-market, ultimately, without good fortune, a mismatch may produce an aberrant gain or loss, maybe causing unpredictable swings in profitability from year to year.

Professional investors do not appreciate this, especially as balance sheet risk still largely goes unvalued in corporate reports. In the age of profit warnings causing share slides of up to 50% or more, managing certainty through the sophisticated use of swaps and other instruments, is a desirable capability.

So, duration can provide a measure of the sensitivity to a change in the general level of interest rates (or the shape of the yield curve), for a given asset or liability, or the balance sheet as a whole. Gap analysis, which evolved around the same time, focuses on the interest rate exposures in a given time period (relevant when considering the incidence of accounting dates).

By 1998, asset/liability modelling had become highly sophisticated. By applying risk return calculations to every decision, cash flow, asset and liability, it is now possible to model the most efficient scenario for the corporation. Interest rates and currencies are more volatile than inflation, but the tools to manage their concomitant risks are now legion.

Foremost among these for the corporate treasurer are swaps - which can turn currency risk into interest rate risk, match interest rate and maturity profiles, improve overall certainty, balance duration, enhance the management of VAR and increase the security of shareholder value. If the balance sheet is actively matched, then this leaves management to focus on the daily commercial decisions relating to supply, production, distribution and sales.

Chapter 13

Corporate Attitudes to Risk

Corporate directors have become more sophisticated in their awareness of risk, but most remain well behind their banking cousins in their awareness of the opportunities and pitfalls related to interest rate and currency risk and the use of hedging techniques and derivatives.

Although they are much less liquid than traded derivatives, such as futures and options, swaps have, since the 1980s, provided the treasurer with the possibility of both matching fixed rate liabilities to assets, but also to move in and out of fixed and floating rate exposures on a view of interest rates. While the risk on a future could theoretically be infinite, the transaction can at least be readily neutralised by a reverse transaction. Liquidity makes this harder in the case of swaps.

Gibsons Greetings in the US and Barings in the UK, may have alerted corporate directors to the dangers of naive or wilful speculation in derivatives. But many who may say they are secure because they never use derivatives, may both be missing opportunities to safely improve returns. Worse still, they could be implicitly speculating the value of the corporation by leaving it exposed to the volatility of interest rates and currencies of existing assets and liabilities, let alone replacements on maturity.

If you or I take the safe course of investing in a five-year government bond to maturity, we may comfort ourselves on the safety of the investment and the security of the return. In 5 years, however, we shall have a cash maturity needing re-investment, where interest rates may be 2% lower, or 5% higher, or the shape of the yield curve has changed. Meanwhile, locked into our 'comfort blanket', we may miss out on the 'ride' in between.

It has been said earlier, that naive neglect can be as costly as active speculation. For those directors who feel unlikely to understand the more esoteric derivatives, swaps offer an understandable, manageable, flexible means to manage balance sheet risk, especially in liabilities, but also in the interest costs and currency values which can impact short-term profitability. Certainty can be achieved without necessarily conceding returns.

Attitudes and usage

In an article in *The Treasurer* in January 1995, Lucy Cassidy of *Record Treasury Management* had surveyed corporates attitudes to and use of derivatives in managing risk. The key findings were:

- 75% of treasurers ranked risk reduction as their prime objective;
- around 90% would use derivatives to manage interest rate and currency risk;
- the main risks in derivatives were their control and complexity;
- 54% felt that sellers of derivatives explained risks poorly or inadequately;

- over 90% would use swaps to manage their risks; the overall approach was mainly 'plain vanilla'.

In 1974, Peter Drucker wrote: "To take risks is the essence of economic activity...the main goal must be to enable companies to take the right risk...by providing knowledge and understanding of the alternative risks."

A growing number of corporates are adopting the VAR approach favoured by bankers. The balance sheet of a bank is of course mainly comprised of financial assets and liabilities, of course. The focus for corporates is around cashflows. Valuation of companies is increasingly being influenced by the ability to generate cash. Swaps can be of substantial use in protecting or enhancing the certainty of cash flows in the home currency.

In *Derivatives for Directors* (ACT, 1995), Richard Cookson said "This, then, should be the objective of good corporate hedging strategy: to stabilise cash flows....Unreliable cash flow projections are not just useless, they are positively dangerous: a company which misjudges the amount it needs to hedge will under- or over-hedge. Either might render it uncompetitive."

Directors may be traditionalist or progressive. Treasuries may take an active or passive approach to managing risk and stabilising cash flows. In foreign exchange transactions, forward contracts will often produce more stability than swaps, while other products may open up the possibility of even greater risk. The use of swaps will need to be couched within the overall business and financial risk management framework.

Directors operate at the strategic end of the company management processes. They should want to set the overall policy for holistic risk management and give guidance as to its implementation. They do not need to see the detail of every hedge transaction, but should be put on enquiry where they have concerns. They will wish to be comforted that the use of swaps to hedge (or especially where used to create) financial risk, is being seen within the overall context of the balance sheet. Otherwise a swap effected to hedge a financial risk in one part of the balance sheet may leave an unmatched exposure in another part.

In 1995, for the first time, BIS members included derivatives in their annual survey of foreign exchange trading. There had been growing concerns at the risks involved. "the notional principal of swap and swap-related positions outstanding surged by 59% last year...Losses faced by end-users in 1994-5 led many corporate customers to review their use of derivative instruments and improve their risk management practices."

However, pre-dating Barings and other examples of misuse, the report concluded: "Growing public recognition of the economic benefits of derivatives markets, a much better understanding of such instruments and more prudent use of them meant that calls for regulatory action...abated. Official initiatives continued to be aimed primarily at improving disclosure standards and promoting closer co-operation and greater management responsibility in the control of risks."

Lessons for all from Barings

There are messages for all corporates in the Barings debacle, not just bankers. Swaps and forwards (including FRAs) may be regarded these days as 'plain vanilla', safe and simple, hedging instruments for the FD to use to improve certainty and control over corporate performance, safeguarding or even enhancing shareholder value.

As well as messages given earlier, the lessons of Barings are pertinent for the corporate user of swaps. There was inadequate separation of function; Leeson was able to approve his own transactions. The reporting systems were either inadequate, incomplete, or unsatisfactorily policed, otherwise how did Leeson exceed his authority to deal. The Directors appear to have had incomplete understanding of what was going on. Even allowing for the fact that a bank is expected to take risks and run open positions, in order to generate profits, the effect of the exposures Leeson had built up was, as we have seen, to 'bet the company'. It failed.

Many corporates world-wide have failed, through a combination of ignorance in the use of derivatives, and/or building up such large speculative positions that the entire net worth of the corporation was on the line. It would not be impossible for a corporate using foreign exchange and interest rate swaps to create such an exposure. As volatility increases, the effect of profit warnings increasingly savages share prices, jobs become less secure, there may be a great temptation to use derivatives in general, swaps in particular, to manage the tactical daily risks.

We have made clear that strategy, an overview and laid down policies, excellent reporting systems and a total balance sheet, asset/liability management type approach are highly recommended in the use of swaps to protect or enhance the certainty of cash flows and corporate profitability, otherwise the opposite may be the consequence.

Chapter 14

Conclusion

S waps have been at the forefront of the phenomenal growth in the use of derivatives. The use and availability of such instruments has greatly enhanced global trade, the understanding of financial risk, the flexibility in managing corporate performance and the success of international banking. Bankers have moved from intermediaries in swap transactions, to counterparties, portfolio holders and traders of swaps and a mind-boggling array of derivatives instruments and products.

Corporates have evolved from using swaps to facilitate medium term funding, to combining them into complex, holistic, financial and business risk management processes. All of these have depended on and resulted in the evolution of computer-based calculation, evaluation, synthesis and modelling systems. It is now possible to value the entire, risk-adjusted, net worth of a corporation at the push of a button.

It should be remembered that there are, essentially four main financial risk management instruments: forwards, swaps, options and futures. Every other derivative will be a combination of one or more of these. An interest rate swap itself is the equivalent of a series of FRAs (forward rate agreements).

There has from time to time been concern from various regulatory and other authorities on the rapid growth in these instruments, in which swaps have been the most significant. It appears to have been generally realised that, with these derivatives largely being 'off-balance sheet' and offshore, transacted in global markets, regulation would be impractical, other than through capital adequacy or reporting constraints.

The volume of outstanding notional principal amounts in, e.g. swaps, dwarfs the volume of outstandings in the underlying instruments. Around 95% of foreign exchange transactions are done for speculative purposes. What has been observed, however, is not just that the volatility of derivatives can often be less than that of interest rates and currencies, but also, they can facilitate the reduction in volatility.

Swaps are here to stay. They are not as complex as many other derivatives. They are widely traded, offering the corporate treasurer and banker alike, more and more flexibility to hedge known risks and facilitate borrowing, even out to 25 years or more.

About the Author

Terry has had two careers. Qualifying as a Chartered Accountant, Banker, Stockbroker and Corporate Treasurer, he followed his professional training by working as an IT Consultant. A 15-year career followed in various aspects of financial services, including a spell as Chief Executive and FD of a major building society. He was involved in the establishment and management of mortgage, savings, insurance, credit card, stockbroking and fund management businesses.

Between 1980 and 1988, he established and directed Treasury and Risk Management functions in two leading financial services providers. During this time he also lectured on these topics, together with Asset/Liability and Total Balance Sheet Management.

In 1991, he was recruited by the now largest NHS Trust in the UK, to resolve its financial problems and establish a Strategic Business Planning function. After three years, the project was complete and his career took a change of direction.

In 1994, he established Hollins Consulting and, after a spell as MD of an International HR and Recruitment Consultancy, he decided to focus on Personal Coaching and Executive Recruitment.

Having integrated NLP Practitioner skills into the business, Terry now works with teams and individuals, in business and in private practice, to facilitate personal growth and development. This is his third book (previously including *The Role of the Finance Director,* FT Pitman 1998); at least two more are planned. He also runs personal development seminars.

He can be reached at Hollins Consulting,
Tel/Fax: 01765 620643
or by Email at: terrycarroll_hollins@lineone.net

Complete Beginner's Guide to the Internet

What exactly is The Internet? Where did it come from and where is it going? And, more importantly, how can everybody take their place in this new community? *The Complete Beginner's Guide to The Internet* tells you: ● What types of resources are available for private, educational and business use, ● What software and hardware you need to access them, ● How to communicate with others, and ● The rules of the Superhighway, known as 'netiquette'. An indispensable guide to the basics of Cyberspace.

128 pages   ISBN:1-873668-62-7   £5.95

Create Your Own Website

Whether it is to showcase your business and its products, or a compilation of information about your favourite hobby or sport, creating your own Web site is very exciting indeed.

This book will help demystify the process of creating and publishing a Web site. Includes what free tools are available, how to create your own dazzling graphics, using a variety of free computer programs and who to talk to when it comes to finding a home for your Web site.

112 pages   ISBN:1-873668-42-2   £5.95

Find What You Want on the Internet

The sheer size of the Internet's information resources is its biggest challenge. There is no central repository of all this information, nor it is catalogued or sorted in ordered fashion.

Find What You Want on The Internet is designed to teach Internet users - from novices to veterans - how to locate information quickly and easily. The book uses jargon-free language, combined with many illustrations. There is also a bonus chapter covering Intelligent Agents

112 pages   ISBN:1-873668-48-1   £5.95

Understand Shares in a Day Second Edition

Shows how the share market really works. Inexperienced investors will learn: ❑ About different types of shares ... ❑ Why share prices fluctuate... ❑ How to read the financial pages ... ❑ How shares are bought and sold ... ❑ How risk can be spread with investment and unit trusts ... ❑ How to build a portfolio of shares ...❑ The risks and rewards associated with Penny Shares

Once this groundwork has been covered, the book explores more complex ideas which will appeal to both beginners and more experienced investors alike.

128 pages   ISBN:1-873668-73-2   £6.95

Understand Bonds & Gilts in a Day 2nd Edition

This handy title shows potential investors, and those with an interest in the bond markets, how to assess the potential risks and rewards, giving a simple to follow set of criteria on which to base investment decisions. Having shown the inexperienced investor how to go about buying bonds, it also teaches even the most arithmetically shy how to calculate the yield on a bond and plan an income based portfolio. The confusing terminology used in the bond market is clearly explained with working definitions of many terms and a comprehensive glossary.

112 pages   ISBN:1-873668-72-4   £6.95

Understand Commodities in a Day

An easy-to-read introduction with plenty of simple examples. It lifts the mysteries of trading in grains, livestock, precious and industrial metals, petroleum, lumber, coffee, sugar, soyabeans, etc.

Having shown the inexperienced investor how to start trading in commodities, it goes on to explain basic strategies used in the markets. Learn... The basic concept of commodity trading... About physical commodity contracts... How to place an executable order in the market... How to analyse commodity markets... Trading strategies from the experts

96 pages   ISBN:1-873668-46-5   £6.95

Understand Derivatives in a Day

Financial derivatives are used as highly-geared vehicles for making money, saving money or preventing its loss. They also have the ability to exploit volatility, guarantee results and avoid taxes. But only if they are used correctly.

Learn...How private investors get started... To Hedge, Straddle and control Risk... Ways to limit the downside but not the upside... About risk free derivative strategies... Trading Psychology - Fear, Hope and Greed... Also, the History of Derivatives; Currency Speculation; Long and Short puts; Tarantula Trading; and much more.

Stefan Bernstein   112 pages
ISBN:1-873668-56-2   £6.95

Understand Financial Risk in a Day

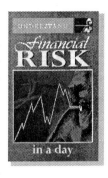

Risk management is all about minimising risks and maximising opportunities. Those who understand what they should be doing, as a result of their risk calculations, will usually come out as winners. Those who flail in the dark will, more often than not, be the losers.

Understand Financial Risk in a Day is a perfect introduction to the subject. Light on detailed formulae and heavy on easy-to-follow examples it will lead the reader to a greater awareness of how to evaluate the risks they are facing and adapt a strategy to create the best possible outcome.

Alex Kiam   96 pages
ISBN:1-873668-24-4   £6.95

Investing in Options: For the Private Investor

A hardback book which shows you exactly how to 'gear' your money to provide more growth. Step-by-step it teaches how you appraise an options position, looking at the rewards and risks, and then how to execute a deal. There are plenty of examples to show you exactly how its done and how to trade profitably.

For the experienced options buyer there are examples of option combinations which can be used to create almost any desired outcome. With options you can make money whichever direction the market is moving.

128 pages   1-873668-59-7   £14.95   Hardback

Successful Spread betting

Spread Betting offers investors a simple and direct way of dealing in the world's financial markets and has significant advantages over other methods of dealing: ...It gives you àccess to financial markets in which you couldn't normally deal without being a registered broker, for example foreign exchange ...Any money you make from Spread Betting is Tax Free ...You can also bet on events and outcomes in the sporting world ...There are no dealing charges - no brokerage or commission fees ...Spread Betting firms offer instant dealing and extended hours so you can take out a position even when the underlying markets are closed.

160 pages   ISBN:1-873668-58-9   £12.95

Timing the Financial Markets:
Charting your way to profit

Shows all levels of investors how to construct charts and graphs of price movements for bonds, shares and commodities. Then it explains, in easy-to-understand language, how to interpret the results and turn them into profit. With computers taking over so much of the trading activity on the world's stockmarkets (news programmes call it "automated trading"), charting is becoming a more and more powerful technique.

96 pages   ISBN:1-873668-47-3   £6.95

International Dictionary of Personal Finance

This dictionary provides a basic vocabulary of terms used in the world of personal finance, from 'A' shares to zero-rating and from accelerated depreciation to yield. Words used in all areas of finance are covered, not just those from basic investment, but also from the arenas of banking, law, national insurance and tax. Both British and American usages are included.

128 pages   ISBN:1-873668-54-6   £6.95

International Dictionary of Derivatives

A dictionary of terms designed to aid all those involved, or about to become involved, with these complex financial instruments. Nothing is missed out, with explanations and diagrams from Accrual Options and Agrigation through to ZEPOs and Zero Gain Collars. Also contains a list of acronyms.

96 pages   ISBN:1-873668-57-0   £6.95

Investing on the Internet

The Internet is revolutionising the way ordinary investors are going about increasing their personal wealth. For the first time everyone can now access information that used to be available only to the investment professionals. And with *Investing on the Internet*, you can be at the forefront of this transformation.

This handy guide will lead you to the best investment tools there are on the web, almost all of which are completely free. Full site addresses are given with a review of content, speed and usefulness.

192 pages   ISBN:1-873668-73-2   £4.95

Investing for the Long Term

This book is aimed at those savvy investors who are content to ride out short term fluctuations in the markets in order to realise bigger long term gains. Be it for school fees, a larger house or retirement, if you need money in more than 10 years time, this book is for you. Very comprehensive; covering everything from growth versus income to understanding company accounts, and from downturns, corrections & crashes to looking at the larger economic picture.

R Linggard 160 pages   ISBN:1-873668-76-7   £14.95   Hardback

Book Ordering

Please complete the form below or use a plain piece of paper and send to:

Europe/Asia
TTL, PO Box 200, Harrogate HG1 2YR, England (or fax to 01423-526035, or email: sales@net-works.co.uk).

USA/Canada
Trafalgar Square, PO Box 257, Howe Hill Road, North Pomfret, Vermont 05053 (or fax to 802-457-1913, call toll free 800-423-4525, or email: tsquare@sover.net)

Postage and handling charge:
UK - £1 for first book, and 50p for each additional book
USA - $5 for first book, and $2 for each additional book (all shipments by UPS, please provide street address).
Elsewhere - £3 for first book, and £1.50 for each additional book via surface post (for airmail and courier rates, please fax or email for a price quote)

Book	Qty	Price

☐ I enclose payment for _____

Postage
Total:

☐ Please debit my Visa/Amex/Mastercard No:

Expiry date: ☐☐☐☐   Signature:

Name: _____

Address: _____

Postcode/Zip: _____

swaps